TOP-RATED
FLOWERIN
SHRUBS
AND HOW TO USE THEM IN YOUR GARDEN

D0752205

This book was produced for Western Publishing Company, Inc., by the staff of Horticultural Associates, Inc., in cooperation with Amfac® Garden Products.

Executive Producer: Richard Ray
Contributing Authors: John Ford, Robert L. Ticknor
Consultants: Claire Barrett, Fred Galle, Ralph Miller, Carl A. Totemeier, Richard Turner, Joseph A. Witt
Photography: Michael Landis
Art Director: Richard Baker
Book Design: Judith Hemmerich
Associate Editors: Michael MacCaskey, Lance Walheim
Research Editor: Randy Peterson
Copy Editors: Greg Boucher, Miriam Boucher
Production Editor: Kathleen Parker
Book Production: Lingke Moeis
Illustrations: Charles Hoeppner, Roy Jones
Typography: Linda Encinas
Additional Photography: William Aplin, Susan A. Roth
Cover Photo: Michael Landis
Acknowledgements: Jim Gibbons, Horticulturist, San Diego Wild Animal Park, Escondido, CA; Chuck Kline, Horticulturist, Sea World, San Diego, CA; Bill Knerr and Robert Ward, Horticulturists, Zoological Society of San Diego, San Diego, CA; Henry Koide, Presidio Garden Center, San Diego, CA; Los Angeles Arboretum; Bill Robinson, Japanese Garden Society of Oregon; Nancy Davidson Short, Seattle, WA; Van Dusen Botanical Display Garden; Van Winden's Nursery, Napa, CA; Whiting's Nursery, St. Helena, CA.

For Western Publishing Company, Inc.:
Editorial Director: Jonathan P. Latimer
Senior Editor: Susan A. Roth
Copy Editor: Karen Stray Nolting

 Golden Press • New York

Western Publishing Company, Inc.

Racine, Wisconsin

Copyright © 1983 by Horticultural Associates, Inc.
All rights reserved. Produced in the U.S.A.
Library of Congress Catalog Card Number 82-81412
Golden® and Golden Press® are trademarks of Western Publishing Company, Inc.
ISBN 0-307-46626-4

Top-Rated Flowering Shrubs

This book is planned to help you select flowering shrubs to serve a variety of landscape uses around your home. Only widely available, dependable plants with a history of proven performance are described.

Defining a shrub: There is no clear-cut distinction in nature between trees and shrubs. People tend to think of trees as tall single-trunked plants and of shrubs as shorter, many-trunked plants. Pruning and training can alter some plants into clearly defined shrubs or trees. Some flowering trees that can serve as shrubs in the landscape are discussed in this book.

Year-round landscape color: Flowering shrubs have different blooming seasons and come in a full spectrum of blossom colors. Many also have colorful fruits or berries, or leaves that turn bright shades in the fall. The photographs in this book can help you visualize how plants can add visual drama to your home's landscape.

Quick plant indentification: To identify a plant you know only by a common name, see the name cross-reference guide on page 63 where the most often used common names are matched with the plant's botanical name, which is used throughout the book.

Where plants will grow: Climate is the strongest factor in determining where a plant will grow successfully. Each growing region has its own native flowering shrubs, but many others are adaptable to that region's growing conditions. The top-rated flowering shrubs for your area are listed in the charts on pages 5 to 7.

Hydrangeas *(Hydrangea sp.)* are widely grown for their large ball-like flower clusters that make a colorful impact in midsummer.

Fuchsia *(Fuchsia sp.)*

Andromeda *(Pieris japonica)*

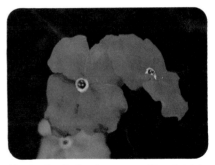

Yesterday-today-tomorrow *(Brunfelsia)*

Aaron's-beard *(Hypericum calycinum)*

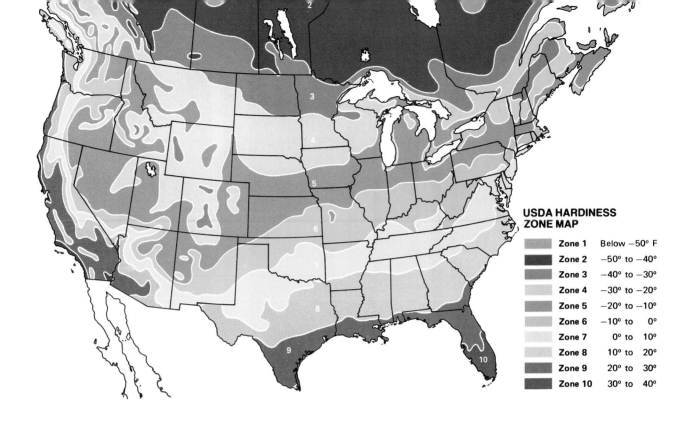

USDA HARDINESS ZONE MAP

	Zone 1	Below −50° F
	Zone 2	−50° to −40°
	Zone 3	−40° to −30°
	Zone 4	−30° to −20°
	Zone 5	−20° to −10°
	Zone 6	−10° to 0°
	Zone 7	0° to 10°
	Zone 8	10° to 20°
	Zone 9	20° to 30°
	Zone 10	30° to 40°

Climates for Flowering Shrubs

The USDA plant hardiness map shows the average low temperatures throughout the United States and Southern Canada. It divides North America into 10 zones with the average minimum temperature of each zone differing by 10 degrees Fahrenheit. All plants in this book are identified in the following charts and in the encyclopedia by the zones where their growth performance has been judged top-rated.

Each plant entry lists the range of zones where the plant is recommended. This indicates the plant's tolerance to both cold and warm climates. For example, *Berberis julianae* is listed for Zones 6-8, and *Berberis thunbergii* is listed for Zones 4-9.

As every gardener learns, cold hardiness is only one factor of a plant's adaptation. A plant's ability to do well in a certain location depends on unique combinations of soil type, wind, rainfall, length and time of cold, humidity, summer temperatures, and temperatures in relation to humidity. For example, one type or another of azalea or rhododendron is hardy enough to survive almost anywhere in the United States. However, these plants require acid soil, which alters their culture in many areas.

The USDA hardiness zone map does not take climate factors other than temperature into consideration. To give you additional information, the map and charts on the following pages break down the United States and Canada into 10 climate regions. For a plant to be adapted to your area, it must be recommended for your USDA hardiness zone and your climate region.

USDA Zones 8 to 10 are particularly complex in the western United States. Many plants with a southern range of Zone 8 can also be grown in Zones 9 and 10 in the West. In these cases, it is best to follow regional recommendations.

The climates around your home: Another aspect of climate important in selecting flowering shrubs is microclimate. Microclimates are the small climates around your home that differ slightly from the general climate of your area. The northern side of your property, which is probably partially shaded most of the day by your house, is a cold microclimate. The southern side of your home, which, unless shaded by trees, receives hot sun almost all day, is a warm microclimate. A good way to become aware of microclimates is to make a site plan. See page 10.

Plants that are borderline hardy for your area may do well if you take protective measures such as providing wind or snow shelters and making use of your property's warm microclimates. It is often possible to grow protected plants successfully in the next colder climate zone.

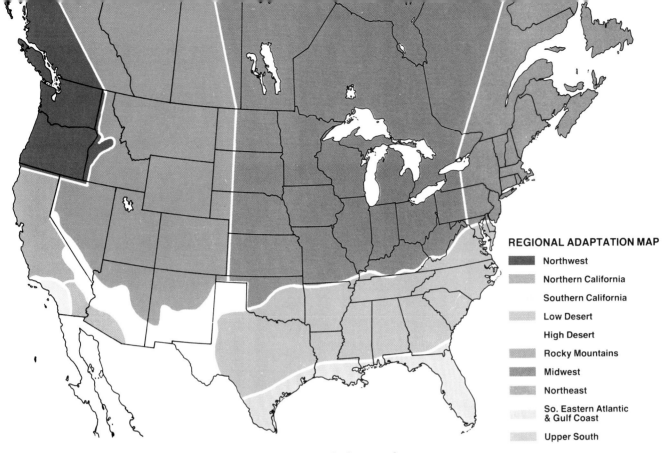

REGIONAL ADAPTATION MAP
- Northwest
- Northern California
- Southern California
- Low Desert
- High Desert
- Rocky Mountains
- Midwest
- Northeast
- So. Eastern Atlantic & Gulf Coast
- Upper South

Regional Adaptation

PLANT NAME	ZONES	NORTHWEST	NORTHERN CALIFORNIA	SOUTHERN CALIFORNIA	LOW DESERT	HIGH DESERT	ROCKY MOUNTAINS	MIDWEST	NORTHEAST	SO. EASTERN ATLANTIC & GULF COAST	UPPER SOUTH
Abelia x grandiflora	6-10	■	■	■	■	■		■	■	■	■
Azalea (See Rhododendron)											
Berberis julianae	6-8	■	■				■	■	■		■
Berberis x mentorensis	5-8	■	■				■	■	■		■
Berberis thunbergii	4-9	■	■				■	■	■		■
Brunfelsia pauciflora 'Floribunda'	8-10		■	■						■	■
Callistemon citrinus	8-10		■	■	■					■	■
Calluna vulgaris	4-7	■	■					■	■		
Camellia japonica	7-10	■	■	■						■	■
Camellia sasanqua	7-10	■	■	■						■	■
Caragana arborescens	2-7	■	■	■	■	■	■	■	■		■
Carissa grandiflora	10		■	■						■	
Chaenomeles sp.	5-9	■	■			■	■	■	■		■
Convolvulus cneorum	7-10		■	■						■	■
Cytisus x praecox	6-9	■	■	■	■			■	■		■
Cytisus racemosus	7-10	■	■	■	■			■	■		■
Cytisus scoparius	6-9	■	■	■				■	■		■
Daphne odora	8-10	■	■	■						■	■
Enkianthus campanulatus	5-9	■	■					■	■		■
Erica carnea	4-8	■	■	■				■	■		■
Erica x darleyensis	4-8	■	■	■				■	■		■

There are many hybrid groups of evergreen azaleas (*Rhododendron* hybrids), each suited to different regions.

Regional Adaptation

PLANT NAME	ZONES	NORTHWEST	NORTHERN CALIFORNIA	SOUTHERN CALIFORNIA	LOW DESERT	HIGH DESERT	ROCKY MOUNTAINS	MIDWEST	NORTHEAST	SO. EASTERN ATLANTIC & GULF COAST	UPPER SOUTH
Escallonia x exoniensis	7-10	■	■	■							
Forsythia x intermedia	5-9	■	■			■	■	■	■		■
Fuchsia x hybrida	9-10	■	■	■						■	
Fuchsia magellanica	6-10	■	■	■			■	■	■	■	■
Gardenia jasminoides	8-10		■	■	■					■	■
Hamamelis x intermedia	6-8	■	■					■	■		■
Hebe sp.	9-10		■	■						■	
Hibiscus rosa-sinensis	9-10		■	■	■					■	
Hibiscus syriacus	5-10	■	■			■	■	■	■	■	■
Hydrangea arborescens	5-9	■	■		■	■	■	■	■	■	■
Hydrangea macrophylla	6-10	■	■	■	■	■		■	■	■	■
Hydrangea paniculata	5-9	■	■			■	■	■	■	■	■
Hydrangea quercifolia	6-9	■	■			■	■	■	■	■	■
Hypericum sp.	5-10	■	■	■		■			■	■	■
Kolkwitzia amabilis	5-8	■		■		■	■	■	■		■
Lagerstroemia indica	7-9	■	■	■	■	■			■	■	■
Lantana sp.	9-10		■	■	■					■	■
Leucothoe fontanesiana	5-8	■	■					■	■		
Lonicera tatarica	3-9	■	■	■			■	■	■		
Mahonia aquifolium	5-9	■	■	■	■	■	■	■	■	■	■
Mahonia bealei	5-10	■	■	■	■	■	■	■	■	■	■
Mahonia lomariifolia	8-10	■	■	■						■	■
Nandina domestica	6-10	■	■	■	■	■			■	■	■
Nerium oleander	8-10		■	■	■	■				■	■
Philadelphus coronarius	5-8	■	■			■	■	■	■		
Philadelphus x lemoinei	5-8	■	■			■	■	■	■		
Philadelphus x virginalis	4-8	■	■			■	■	■	■		
Photinia x fraseri	7-10	■	■	■	■	■				■	■
Pieris sp.	5-9	■	■				■	■	■		■
Pittosporum tobira	8-10	■	■	■	■	■				■	■

In mild climates camellias *(Camellia sp.)* bear lovely blossoms for many months in fall and winter; glossy, evergreen foliage is attractive year-round.

Regional Adaptation

PLANT NAME	ZONES	NORTHWEST	NORTHERN CALIFORNIA	SOUTHERN CALIFORNIA	LOW DESERT	HIGH DESERT	ROCKY MOUNTAINS	MIDWEST	NORTHEAST	SO. EASTERN ATLANTIC & GULF COAST	UPPER SOUTH
Potentilla fruticosa	2-9	■	■	■	■	■	■	■	■	■	■
Prunus caroliniana	7-10		■	■	■	■			■	■	
Prunus x cistena	2-9	■	■	■		■	■	■	■		■
Prunus laurocerasus	7-10	■	■					■	■	■	■
Pyracantha angustifolia	5-9	■	■	■	■	■					■
Pyracantha coccinea	5-9	■	■	■	■	■		■		■	■
Pyracantha koidzumii	7-10	■	■	■	■	■		■			■
Pyracantha 'Tiny Tim'	7-9	■	■	■	■	■		■	■		■
Raphiolepis indica	8-10	■	■	■	■	■				■	■
Rhododendron hybrids*	4-10	■	■					■	■	■	■
Rosa hybrids	5-10	■	■	■	■	■	■	■	■	■	■
Rosmarinus officinalis	7-10	■	■	■	■	■			■	■	■
Sarcococca hookerana humilis	7-10	■	■	■					■		■
Skimmia japonica	6-8	■	■						■		■
Spartium junceum	7-10	■	■	■	■	■					
Spiraea x bumalda	3-9	■	■				■	■	■	■	■
Spiraea japonica	6-9	■	■				■	■	■	■	■
Spiraea prunifolia	5-9	■	■				■	■	■	■	■
Spiraea x vanhouttei	5-9	■	■				■	■	■	■	■
Syringa x chinensis	4-7	■	■			■	■	■	■		■
Syringa vulgaris	3-8	■	■			■	■	■	■		■
Trachelospermum asiaticum	7-10	■	■	■	■	■				■	■
Trachelospermum jasminoides	8-10	■	■	■	■	■				■	■
Viburnum x burkwoodii	5-10	■	■	■			■	■	■		■
Viburnum davidii	7-10	■	■	■						■	■
Viburnum opulus	3-10	■	■	■			■	■	■	■	■
Viburnum plicatum	4-9	■	■	■			■	■	■	■	■
Viburnum tinus	7-10	■	■	■	■					■	■
Viburnum trilobum	2-9	■	■			■	■	■	■		■
Weigela sp.	4-9	■	■			■	■	■	■		■

*See pages 43 to 45 for zone information on azaleas and rhododendrons.

Using Flowering Shrubs in Your Garden

Flowering shrubs have a double personality in the landscape. They are first of all appreciated for the beauty of their blossoms, but when out of bloom they become structural features of the landscape as are non-flowering shrubs. They are backbone plants around the house and in the garden, defining boundaries, softening architecture, and providing privacy and greenery.

The following examples demonstrate the usefulness of flowering shrubs.

LANDSCAPE USES

Accent: When in bloom, a flowering shrub draws the eye, creating a focal point or accent in that part of the garden.

Barrier plant: Flowering shrubs with thorns or very dense growth are often used to keep people and animals from going where you don't want them to go.

Border planting: The perimeter of a yard is frequently bordered with shrubs. Planting beds with curving contours rather than straight lines are more visually appealing.

Concealing: Shrubs have long been used to camouflage unattractive water meters and spigots on the sides of houses, as well as to section-off an area of the yard as a work or utility area.

Container plants: Many flowering shrubs thrive in tight quarters, making it possible to grow them in tubs or containers to decorate a deck, patio, or porch.

Planting flowering shrubs that bloom in different seasons creates a colorful landscape throughout the year.

Hydrangea *(Hydrangea sp.)*

Oleander *(Nerium oleander)*

'Coral Bells' azalea *(Rhododendron)*

Carolina cherry laurel *(Prunus sp.)*

Large-flowered hydrangeas *(Hydrangea sp.)* make dramatic accent plants.

Spiraea *(Spiraea sp.)* makes an excellent fine-textured hedge.

David viburnum *(Viburnum davidii)* has interesting foliage and white flower clusters followed by turquoise-colored fruit.

Definition: Flowering shrubs can be used to emphasize the shape or size of an area. A low hedge surrounding a patio accentuates its position in the landscape. Shrubs planted on either side of a door or pathway provide framing that directs the eye.

Entryways: Plants used around an entrance of a home serve as part of its welcome mat, inviting visitors to approach the door. Many flowering shrubs are attractive and colorful year-round—just what you want to frame your front door.

Foundation planting: Shrubs are traditionally used in either formal or informal designs to decorate the front of a house and conceal the house's foundation. Evergreen shrubs, either flowering or non-flowering, are most suitable.

Ground covers: Low-growing, ground-hugging shrubs can form a colorful carpet in large or small areas. They help prevent erosion on steep slopes without blocking a view, and require less care than a lawn.

Hedge: Fine-textured shrubs make the best-looking hedges. They can be pruned into a neat shape for a *formal* hedge or allowed to assume their natural shape for an *informal* hedge. Use a hedge as a low barrier, to act as a living fence, or to mark the boundary of your property.

Sketching a site plan of your property, similar to the example shown below, helps you identify your landscape needs. Once you note which views should be blocked or preserved, where shade is needed, areas of poor soil or bad drainage, and paths of movement, you can begin to choose plants that meet your specific landscape requirements.

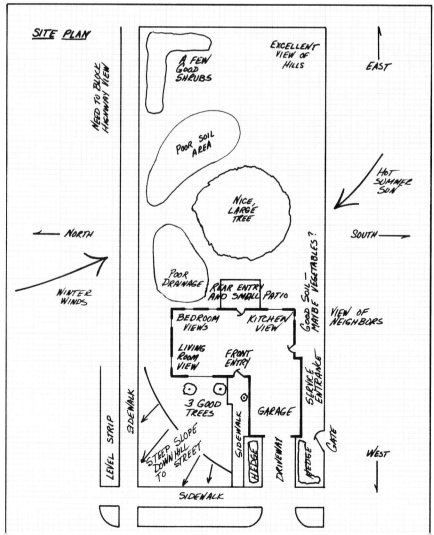

Many flowering shrubs that are fussy about soil conditions can be grown successfully in raised planting beds or containers, where it is easy to amend the soil to satisfy their needs. In cold climates some frost-sensitive flowering shrubs can be grown outdoors in containers during the summer, if they are brought inside to winter-over.

Late color: Flowering shrubs are usually thought of as spring-blooming plants, but many of them bloom throughout the summer. Coordinated with your other plants, they can add continuous color to your garden. Many deciduous shrubs offer glowing autumn foliage and bright berries that can last well into winter.

Privacy: Some flowering shrubs can serve as excellent clipped or unclipped hedges or screens.

Soften architectural lines: Planted alongside a building, shrubs help blend it into the landscape, giving the structure a permanent look.

Specimen: A shrub with an unusual or distinctive growth habit or flower form can be planted standing alone in the midst of a lawn or ground cover planting.

Stopgap-filler: Quick-growing shrubs can cover a space in the garden created by an unexpected plant loss.

Transition: A low island planting of flowering shrubs can form a colorful visual transition and a physical barrier between parts of the yard and garden.

SITE PLAN

A site plan is a sketch or diagram, drawn to scale, of your house and yard. It shows the locations of doors, windows, and rooms, as well as trees, shrubs, garden beds, and outdoor areas such as patios and walks. Other physical characteristics of your property that might affect your gardening efforts should also be noted—good and bad views from indoors and out, directions of prevailing winds, slopes, sun patterns, and high and low spots.

Done properly, a site plan takes a good deal of time and observation. You should watch how the sun and wind patterns change with the seasons. These observations are important since some areas of your property may be in full sun in winter but be shaded in summer. Noting the growing conditions of different areas of your yard will help you choose the trees and shrubs that will serve you best and be most trouble-free.

You can make an accurate site plan using graph paper and a copy of your survey. Record landscape features not noted on the survey, such as trees and garden plots, by carefully measuring their distances from the house. Mark trees and shrubs with circles indicating their branch spread at maturity. When you have a good diagram of your property, you can place tracing paper over it and experiment with possible planting and landscaping ideas before you ever touch a shovel to the ground.

Cranberry bush *(Viburnum opulus)* is a deciduous shrub that is noted for its flowers, foliage, and berries.

Selecting flowering shrubs that bloom in different seasons can ensure a colorful landscape year-round.

Trailing lantana *(Lantana montevidensis)* makes a colorful border plant.

PHYSICAL CHARACTERISTICS

When making final plant selections you'll want to consider such physical characteristics as: whether the shrub should be evergreen or deciduous; its shape, size, and texture; growth rate; maintenance needs; and season of bloom.

Evergreen or deciduous: Broadleaved, flowering evergreens retain their greenery year-round and thus give a landscape a strong structure all year. Deciduous shrubs, when leafless, appear lighter and airier. Most gardens benefit from a mixture of evergreen and deciduous shrubs. Use evergreens where year-round camouflage or privacy is important.

Habit: All shrubs have individual growth characteristics. Some grow tall and vase-shaped, others low and wide. Choose ones whose shape and size best enhance your setting. Natural tendencies may be encouraged, or modified, but a good deal of work can be eliminated by choosing a shrub whose natural growth habits fit the site.

The texture of a shrub is an important feature of its landscape impact. Dainty, delicate leaves and flowers can make a small area seem larger, a close area farther away. Heavy-textured, large leaves will make a large area seem smaller and a distant area closer. The size, shape, and texture of leaves, and whether the flowers are large and bright or small and pastel determines how a shrub blends in with other plants.

Rate of growth: If you want an immediate effect, choose fast-growing shrubs. However, keep in mind that some fast growers have nasty habits such as invasive roots, open leggy growth, or excessive litter.

Maintenance: Certain shrubs require less pruning, watering, or spraying than others. See pages 60-62 to see how much care a particular shrub requires.

Blossoms: Season of bloom and flower color are obviously important. Most flowering shrubs bloom in spring, but there are also summer-flowering shrubs and shrubs that scatter bloom throughout the year. Many flowering shrubs offer more than one color.

Flower colors can have strikingly different effects on the landscape. White is a natural choice to lighten up shaded areas and to harmonize with other, brightly blooming plants. Blue is a cool, soothing color. Yellows and reds are generally vibrant, warm colors that can make a cool spot seem warm—or a hot area even hotter.

Choose flower colors with a painter's eye. Use them to complement and blend with other blooming plants. When choosing flower colors keep the color of your house in mind. For instance, planting a blue-flowering hydrangea against the foundation of a blue house would lessen the impact of the flowers, while the same shrub would be nicely highlighted against a white house.

Additional features: Once you realize what kind of shrub you need, look for additional ornamental bonuses. Fall foliage color, brightly colored fruit, or colorful new growth can make a shrub a beautiful addition to the garden long after the flowers have faded.

SELECTION AID

The lists of shrubs that follow will help you choose plants most suitable for specific landscape purposes. They describe shrubs that solve problems, have specific attractions, or fit into difficult locations.

Use these lists as an introduction to the descriptions of shrubs in the plant encyclopedia section, but do not decide on any shrub until you have read its complete description. If a shrub is listed without a specific species, such as *Hebe sp.,* it means there are several species to select from. To choose wisely, you must go to the individual plant description for full information.

Entryways are special landscape situations that call for plants that are attractive all year and that have outstanding features in different seasons. Evergreen flowering shrubs add color excitement when in bloom; provide consistent year-round greenery.

It is easy to amend the soil in raised planting beds, making it feasible to grow shrubs that require a different type of soil than you have in your garden.

Mock orange *(Philadelphus sp.)*

Lantana *(Lantana sp.)*

Lemon bottlebrush *(Callistemon citrinus)*

Flowering Shrubs Landscape Use Lists

White Blossoms

		Zones
Abelia x grandiflora	Glossy Abelia	6-10
Calluna vulgaris	Scotch Heather	4-7
Camellia sp.	Camellia	7-10
Carissa grandiflora	Natal Plum	10
Chaenomeles sp.	Flowering Quince	5-9
Convolvulus cneorum	Bush Morning-Glory	7-10
Cytisus sp.	Broom	6-10
Daphne odora	Winter Daphne	8-10
Fuchsia sp.	Fuchsia	6-10
Gardenia jasminoides	Gardenia	8-10
Hebe menziesii	Hebe	9-10
Hibiscus sp.	Hibiscus	5-10
Hydrangea sp.	Hydrangea	5-10
Lagerstroemia indica	Crape Myrtle	7-9
Leucothoe fontanesiana	Drooping Leucothoe	5-8
Lonicera tatarica 'Alba'	White Tatarian Honeysuckle	3-9
Nandina domestica	Heavenly Bamboo	6-10
Nerium oleander	Oleander	8-10
Philadelphus sp.	Mock Orange	4-8
Photinia x fraseri	Red-Tip Photinia	7-10
Pieris japonica	Lily-of-the-Valley Shrub	5-9
Pittosporum tobira	Tobira	8-10
Potentilla fruticosa	Shrubby Cinquefoil	2-9
Prunus sp.	Flowering Fruit	2-10
Pyracantha sp.	Firethorn	5-10

White Blossoms (continued)

		Zones
Raphiolepis indica	Indian Hawthorn	8-10
Rhododendron hybrids	Azalea and Rhododendron	4-10
Rosa hybrids	Rose	5-10
Sarcococca hookerana humilis	Sweet Box	7-10
Skimmia japonica	Skimmia	6-8
Spiraea sp.	Spiraea	3-9
Syringa vulgaris	Common Lilac	3-8
Trachelospermum sp.	Star Jasmine	7-10
Viburnum sp.	Viburnum	2-10
Weigela sp.	Weigela	4-9

Orange or Coral Blossoms

		Zones
Chaenomeles sp.	Flowering Quince	5-9
Hibiscus rosa-sinensis	Chinese Hibiscus	9-10
Lantana sp.	Lantana	9-10
Rhododendron hybrids	Azalea and Rhododendron	4-10
Rosa hybrids	Rose	5-10

Red Blossoms

		Zones
Callistemon citrinus	Lemon Bottlebrush	8-10
Camellia sp.	Camellia	7-10
Chaenomeles sp.	Flowering Quince	5-9
Erica carnea	Spring Heath	4-8
Fuchsia sp.	Fuchsia	6-10
Hibiscus sp.	Hibiscus	5-10
Hydrangea sp.	Hydrangea	5-10
Kolkwitzia amabilis	Beautybush	5-8
Lagerstroemia indica	Crape Myrtle	7-9
Lantana sp.	Lantana	9-10
Lonicera tatarica zabelii	Tatarian Honeysuckle	3-9
Nerium oleander	Oleander	8-10
Potentilla fruticosa	Shrubby Cinquefoil	2-9
Rhododendron hybrids	Azalea and Rhododendron	4-10
Rosa hybrids	Rose	5-10
Spiraea sp.	Spiraea	3-9
Syringa vulgaris	Common Lilac	3-8
Weigela sp.	Weigela	4-9

Shrubby cinquefoil *(Potentilla fruticosa)*

Hibiscus *(Hibiscus rosa-sinensis)*

Lilac *(Syringa vulgaris)*

Yellow Blossoms

		Zones
Berberis sp.	Barberry	4-9
Caragana arborescens	Siberian Pea Shrub	2-7
Cytisus sp.	Broom	6-10
Enkianthus campanulatus	Enkianthus	5-9
Forsythia x intermedia	Border Forsythia	5-9
Hamamelis x intermedia	Witch Hazel	6-8
Hibiscus rosa-sinensis	Chinese Hibiscus	9-10
Hypericum sp.	St. John's-Wort	5-10
Lantana sp.	Lantana	9-10
Mahonia sp.	Mahonia	5-10
Nerium oleander	Oleander	8-10
Potentilla fruticosa	Shrubby Cinquefoil	2-9
Rhododendron hybrids	Azalea and Rhododendron	4-10
Rosa hybrids	Rose	5-10
Spartium junceum	Spanish Broom	7-10

Pink Flowers

		Zones
Abelia x grandiflora	Glossy Abelia	6-10
Calluna vulgaris	Scotch Heather	4-7
Camellia sp.	Camellia	7-10
Chaenomeles sp.	Flowering Quince	5-9
Daphne odora	Winter Daphne	8-10
Erica sp.	Heath	4-8
Escallonia x exoniensis	Escallonia	7-10
Fuchsia sp.	Fuchsia	6-10
Hibiscus sp.	Hibiscus	5-10
Hydrangea sp.	Hydrangea	5-10
Kolkwitzia amabilis	Beautybush	5-8
Lagerstroemia indica	Crape Myrtle	7-9
Lantana sp.	Lantana	9-10
Lonicera tatarica	Tatarian Honeysuckle	3-9
Nerium oleander	Oleander	8-10
Raphiolepis indica	Indian Hawthorn	8-10
Rhododendron hybrids	Azalea and Rhododendron	4-10
Rosa hybrids	Rose	5-10
Spiraea sp.	Spiraea	3-9
Syringa vulgaris	Common Lilac	3-8
Weigela sp.	Weigela	4-9

Blue to Purple Blossoms

		Zones
Brunfelsia pauciflora 'Floribunda'	Yesterday-Today-and-Tomorrow	8-10
Calluna vulgaris	Scotch Heather	4-7
Chaenomeles sp.	Flowering Quince	5-9
Erica x darleyensis	Darley Heath	4-8
Fuchsia sp.	Fuchsia	6-10
Hebe sp.	Hebe	9-10
Hibiscus sp.	Hibiscus	5-10
Hydrangea sp.	Hydrangea	5-10
Kolkwitzia amabilis	Beautybush	5-8
Lagerstroemia indica	Crape Myrtle	7-9
Lantana sp.	Lantana	9-10
Rhododendron hybrids	Azalea and Rhododendron	4-10
Rosa hybrids	Rose	5-10
Rosmarinus officinalis	Rosemary	7-10
Syringa vulgaris	Common Lilac	3-8

Heavenly bamboo *(Nandina domestica)*

Burkwood viburnum *(Viburnum x burkwoodii)*

Tobira *(Pittosporum tobira)*

Summer-Flowering Shrubs

Summer-flowering shrubs bring color to the landscape long after the first burst of bloom in spring. Many bloom into the fall.

		Zones
Abelia x grandiflora	Glossy Abelia	6-10
Callistemon citrinus	Lemon Bottlebrush	8-10
Carissa grandiflora	Natal Plum	10
Fuchsia sp.	Fuchsia	6-10
Hibiscus sp.	Hibiscus	5-10
Hydrangea sp.	Hydrangea	5-10
Hypericum calycinum	Aaron's-Beard	5-10
Lagerstroemia indica	Crape Myrtle	7-9
Lantana sp.	Lantana	9-10
Lonicera tatarica	Tatarian Honeysuckle	3-9
Nandina domestica	Heavenly Bamboo	6-10
Nerium oleander	Oleander	8-10
Potentilla fruticosa	Shrubby Cinquefoil	2-9
Rosa hybrids	Rose	5-10
Spartium junceum	Spanish Broom	7-10
Spiraea sp.	Spiraea	3-9
Trachelospermum sp.	Star Jasmine	7-10

Fragrant Blossoms

These shrubs please the nose as well as the eye. Some must be enjoyed up close, others will perfume an entire garden.

		Zones
Carissa grandiflora	Natal Plum	10
Cytisus sp.	Broom	6-10
Daphne odora	Winter Daphne	8-10
Gardenia jasminoides	Gardenia	8-10
Hamamelis x intermedia	Witch Hazel	6-8
Lonicera tatarica	Tatarian Honeysuckle	3-9
Philadelphus sp.	Mock Orange	4-8
Pittosporum tobira	Tobira	8-10
Rhododendron hybrids	Azalea and Rhododendron	4-10
Rosa hybrids	Rose	5-10
Sarcococca hookerana humilis	Sweet Box	7-10
Spartium junceum	Spanish Broom	7-10
Syringa sp.	Lilac	3-8
Trachelospermum sp.	Star Jasmine	7-10
Viburnum sp.	Viburnum	2-10

Clipped Hedges

These are shrubs that respond well to frequent shearing. Use them where a formal hedge is desired. However, keep in mind that frequent pruning often reduces flowering.

		Zones
Abelia x grandiflora	Glossy Abelia	6-10
Berberis sp.	Barberry	4-9
Callistemon citrinus	Lemon Bottlebrush	8-10
Camellia sp.	Camellia	7-10
Carissa grandiflora	Natal Plum	10
Chaenomeles sp.	Flowering Quince	5-9
Forsythia x intermedia	Border Forsythia	5-9
Lonicera tatarica	Tatarian Honeysuckle	3-9
Photinia x fraseri	Red-Tip Photinia	7-10
Pittosporum tobira	Tobira	8-10
Pyracantha sp.	Firethorn	5-10
Rosmarinus officinalis	Rosemary	7-10
Viburnum sp.	Viburnum	2-10

For Barriers

These shrubs can be used to keep people and animals from going where you don't want them to. All are dense and most have thorns.

		Zones
Berberis sp.	Barberry	4-9
Carissa grandiflora	Natal Plum	10
Chaenomeles sp.	Flowering Quince	5-9
Mahonia sp.	Mahonia	5-10
Pyracantha sp.	Firethorn	5-10
Rosa hybrids	Rose	5-10

Red Japanese barberry (*Berberis thunbergii* 'Atropurpurea')

Hydrangea (*Hydrangea macrophylla*)

Aaron's-beard (*Hypericum calycinum*)

Color in More Than One Season

With any combination of flowers, fruit, foliage, or interesting bark, these shrubs are highlights in the landscape for many months of the year.

		Zones
Abelia x grandiflora		
	Glossy Abelia	6-10
Berberis sp.	Barberry	4-9
Callistemon citrinus		
	Lemon Bottlebrush	8-10
Carissa grandiflora	Natal Plum	10
Enkianthus campanulatus		
	Enkianthus	5-9
Hamamelis x intermedia		
	Witch Hazel	6-8
Kolkwitzia amabilis		
	Beautybush	5-8
Lagerstroemia indica		
	Crape Myrtle	7-9
Mahonia sp.	Mahonia	5-10
Nandina domestica		
	Heavenly Bamboo	6-10
Photinia x fraseri		
	Red-Tip Photinia	7-10
Pittosporum tobira	Tobira	8-10
Pyracantha sp.	Firethorn	5-10
Raphiolepis indica		
	Indian Hawthorn	8-10
Rhododendron hybrids		
	Deciduous Azaleas	5-8
Rosa hybrids	Rose	5-10
Sarcococca hookerana humilis		
	Sweet Box	7-10
Skimmia japonica	Skimmia	6-8
Viburnum sp.	Viburnum	2-10

Grow in Containers

These well-behaved shrubs are adapted to container growing. Attractive over a long period, they are perfect companions for patio or porch. Container growing allows you to grow tender species in cold climates where plants are easily moved to protected sites during cold weather.

		Zones
Calluna vulgaris		
	Scotch Heather	4-7
Camellia sp.	Camellia	7-10
Fuchsia sp.	Fuchsia	6-10
Gardenia jasminoides		
	Gardenia	8-10
Hibiscus rosa-sinensis		
	Chinese Hibiscus	9-10
Hydrangea sp.	Hydrangea	5-10
Lagerstroemia indica		
	Crape Myrtle	7-9
Lantana sp.	Lantana	9-10
Leucothoe fontanesiana		
	Drooping Leucothoe	5-8
Mahonia sp.	Mahonia	5-10
Nandina domestica		
	Heavenly Bamboo	6-10
Photinia x fraseri		
	Red-Tip Photinia	7-10
Pieris japonica		
	Lily-of-the-Valley Shrub	5-9
Pittosporum tobira	Tobira	8-10
Rhododendron hybrids		
	Azalea and Rhododendron	4-10
Rosmarinus officinalis		
	Rosemary	7-10
Skimmia japonica	Skimmia	6-8
Trachelospermum sp.		
	Star Jasmine	7-10

Ground Covers

These are low, mostly spreading plants which can be used as colorful ground covers. If specific species or cultivars are not listed, choose low, compact, or spreading types.

		Zones
Abelia x grandiflora 'Prostrata'		
	Prostrate Glossy Abelia	6-10
Berberis thunbergii 'Crimson Pygmy'		
	Crimson Pygmy Barberry	4-9
Calluna vulgaris		
	Scotch Heather	4-7
Camellia sasanqua		
	Sasanqua Camellia	7-10
Carissa grandiflora	Natal Plum	10
Erica x darleyensis		
	Darley Heath	4-8
Hypericum calycinum		
	Aaron's-Beard	5-10
Lantana sp.	Lantana	9-10
Pyracantha sp.	Firethorn	5-10
Raphiolepis indica		
	Indian Hawthorn	8-10
Rosmarinus officinalis		
	Rosemary	7-10
Sarcococca hookerana humilis		
	Sweet Box	7-10
Trachelospermum sp.		
	Star Jasmine	7-10

A Guide to Top-Rated Flowering Shrubs

The flowering shrubs described in the following encyclopedia section are considered top-rated garden plants because of their reliable performance in many areas of the United States. These shrubs are readily available in nurseries and garden centers in the climate zones indicated in the plant listing.

Encyclopedia entries: The following descriptive entries are arranged alphabetically by the botanical name of the plant genus. For quick identification, the most widely used common names are shown in large, dark type just below the genus name. The top-rated flowering shrubs belonging to the genus are then described.

Each entry includes the climate zone in which the shrub will grow well, its potential height, and whether the plant is evergreen or deciduous. The growth habit of the shrub, size and color of flowers, and other special characteristics, such as leaf size and texture, bark, fruits and berries, are discussed. Any cultivars or hybrids selected as proven performers are also described. Soil requirements, best planting sites, long-term care information, and any troublesome pest problems are discussed.

Planning aids: Individual plant entries discuss ways each flowering shrub can be used most effectively in your garden. The accompanying photographs help you visualize how the mature flowering shrub would look in your garden. The photographs illustrate both common and uncommon ways flowering shrubs are used in a variety of landscaping situations.

Spiraea *(Spiraea sp.)* is widely adapted; adds vivid color to landscape in late spring or early summer.

'Tempo' rose *(Rosa hybrid)*

Viburnum *(Viburnum sp.)*

Hibiscus *(Hibiscus rosa-sinensis)*

Indian hawthorn *(Raphiolepis indica)*

Glossy abelia *(Abelia x grandiflora)* blooms in summer; has purplish foliage in fall.

Red Japanese barberry *(Berberis thunbergii* 'Atropurpurea') has colorful foliage. Barberry berries shown below.

Abelia x grandiflora
Glossy Abelia
Zones: 6-10. To 6 feet.
Deciduous or evergreen.

Glossy abelia is the most popular and hardiest abelia. Evergreen in the South; deciduous in the North. Leaves are glossy green, turning bronze-purple in fall. Abundant small white or pink-tinged flowers bloom all summer until fall frost. Use this fine-textured shrub in borders or as a pruned or unpruned hedge.

Can be grown in Zone 5 on a well-protected site. Abelias flower more profusely in full sun but will grow in partial shade.

Several cultivars are available: 'Edward Goucher' is a compact shrub that bears lilac-pink flowers from early summer until fall frost; 'Prostrata', a prostrate form seldom exceeding 2 feet and somewhat more tender than the species, makes an excellent ground cover; 'Sherwoodii' is a dwarf cultivar that may reach 3 feet.

Azalea

(See *Rhododendron* hybrids)

Berberis
Barberry
There are nearly 500 species in this genus, native over a wide area of the world. Some species are deciduous, others evergreen, while some are evergreen in warmer areas and deciduous in the North. Most are thorny shrubs with yellow wood. Deciduous types usually have brightly colored foliage in autumn.

Grown as ornamentals for their small rounded leaves, barberries have yellow, or occasionally red, flowers and yellow, red, or black berries. They are spiny and are good barrier or hedge plants. Barberries withstand pruning or shearing and can easily be trained into an attractive screen or hedge.

Berberis julianae
Wintergreen Barberry
Zones: 6-8. To 10 feet.
Evergreen.

This handsome plant has lustrous, dark green foliage, yellow flowers in spring, and dark bluish-black berries in autumn. Wintergreen barberry is very thorny with triple spines on stems and spiny teeth on the evergreen leaves, making it an excellent barrier plant. Also makes an attractive specimen shrub, planted in solitary splendor. The cultivar 'Nana' is a smaller-growing plant, to 3 or 4 feet tall, good used in mixed foundation plantings. 'Pyramidalis' has a pyramidal shape and is a useful specimen shrub.

Berberis x mentorensis
Mentor Barberry
Zones: 5-8. To 6-8 feet.
Evergreen to semideciduous.

This barberry is evergreen in mild climates but deciduous in colder zones during severe winters, often holding its leaves only until Christmas. Tolerates heat and drought better than most barberries, making it one of the best for growing in the Midwest. This highly regarded hedge plant can also be used as a specimen shrub, in mass plantings, shrub borders, or in foundation plantings. Space 15 to 18 inches apart for a hedge.

Berberis thunbergii
Japanese Barberry
Zones: 4-9. To 7 feet.
Deciduous.

This very hardy shrub may grow into Zone 3 on protected sites. Grows upright. The dense branches are covered with roundish, green leaves that turn red in autumn. Bears yellow flowers tinged with red, as large as 1/2 inch in diameter. Brilliant red berries appear in a heavy set in fall and may last into winter. This tough shrub will grow under adverse conditions, thriving in most soils, in sun or partial shade, and tolerating dry conditions once established. Widely used in hedges or as a barrier plant,

Japanese barberry also makes a good specimen plant.

A number of cultivars have been selected. Red Japanese barberry, 'Atropurpurea', is not quite as hardy as the species; leaves are bright bronze-red when grown in full sunlight, green if grown in the shade; grows to 5 feet tall. Crimson pygmy Japanese barberry, 'Atropurpurea Nana', has a dwarf, very compact growth habit, to 2 feet tall; dark red summer foliage turns amber with cool weather; almost as hardy as the species; use as a specimen plant in rock gardens or as low hedging.

Brunfelsia pauciflora 'Floribunda'
Yesterday-Today-and-Tomorrow
Zones: 8-10. To 10 feet.
Evergreen.

This colorful shrub is native to Brazil. The dark green leaves are 4 inches long and can be slightly twisted.

Tubular-shaped blossoms, borne in clusters, appear profusely in spring and early summer. They open purple, turn lavender and then white, hence the common name. Should be pruned in spring to shape shrub and remove scraggly branches. Plant in a fertile, well-drained soil and protect from direct sunlight. Excellent in containers.

Callistemon citrinus
Lemon Bottlebrush
Zones: 8-10. To 8-10 feet.
Evergreen.

The lemon bottlebrush forms a tall, rounded shrub, but is sometimes pruned into a tree. The foliage is narrow and can vary from 1 to 3 inches long. It is copper-colored as it emerges, becoming bright green with maturity. Bright red flower clusters are 2 to 6 inches long with 1-inch-long stamens that resemble the bristles of a brush. Heaviest bloom is in the spring and summer but scattered flowering occurs

The unusual flowers of yesterday-today-and-tomorrow *(Brunfelsia pauciflora* 'Floribunda') open purple (shown below), turn lavender and then white.

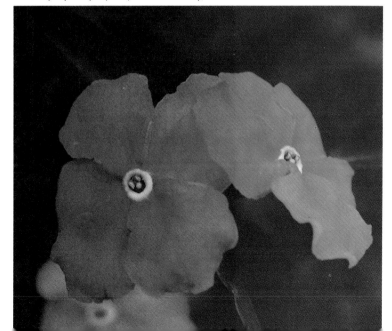

21

Scotch heather (Calluna vulgaris) bears spikes of flowers in late summer and makes a good ground cover.

Japanese camellia (Camellia japonica) is a favorite as a specimen, hedge, or screen. Blossoms, shown below, are borne for many months.

throughout the year. Seed capsules are ovoid and remain on the plant for several years.

The common name of this species refers to the citrus odor emitted by the leaves when crushed.

Lemon bottlebrush is drought-tolerant but grows best in a moist, well-drained soil. Alkaline and saline conditions are tolerated. Use as a specimen plant, screen, espalier, or informal hedge.

Calluna vulgaris

Scotch Heather

Zones: 4-7. To 1-3 feet.
Evergreen.

This flowering shrub is native from Iceland to Turkey and to North Africa. Heather is eye-catching as a specimen in rock gardens and shrub borders, used as a ground cover or potted plant, and provides cut flowers, fresh or dried.

Usually grows 1 to 2 feet tall with tiny, scalelike, dense dark green leaves and spikes of small purplish-pink bell-shaped flowers, which open from July to September. However, growth characteristics are variable.

Camellia

Camellia

This genus contains about 80 species of evergreen shrubs and small trees native to eastern and southeastern Asia. They are plants for warm areas, not able to withstand sub-zero temperatures. Some are severely damaged by heavy frosts. Camellia is Alabama's state flower.

Camellias are grown for their showy, waxy flowers, which may be single or double, measure from 2 to 5 inches across, and come in a range of colors from white to pink to red. The leaves are glossy dark green and are attractive year-round.

Most camellias demand a moist but well-drained, slightly acid soil, rich in organic matter. Too much, or too little, water can cause problems and they cannot be planted too deeply. If the base of the trunk is covered by soil, plants will not

thrive. Camellias benefit from a 2-inch-thick mulch that keeps roots cool and aids in controlling rapid changes of the moisture content of soil. These shrubs do well in light shade, blooming prolifically where other shrubs would flower only sparsely.

Camellias are often grown in containers in regions colder than their hardiness zone and brought inside during cold weather. They are also grown in greenhouses.

Camellias are of special interest to many gardeners, and over 3,000 different cultivars have been selected.

Camellia japonica
Japanese Camellia
Zones: 7-10. To 15-45 feet.
Evergreen.

The most commonly grown camellia, this species is a beautiful specimen or border shrub. It is effective as a clipped hedge or screen, and grows well in containers. Blooms for several months anytime between October and May, depending upon the variety and the climate. There are over 2,000 named cultivars.

Camellia sasanqua
Sasanqua Camellia
Zones: 7-10. To 15 feet.
Evergreen.

Blooming season begins in fall or early winter, just before that of the Japanese camellia. Plant habit varies from an erect shrub to spreading and vinelike forms. This camellia can be used as a hedge, ground cover, espalier, or screen, and grows well in containers. Over 75 cultivars have been named.

Caragana arborescens

Siberian Pea Shrub, Pea Tree

Zones: 2-7. To 15 feet.
Evergreen.

Native to Manchuria, this pea shrub was first brought to North America in the mid 1700's and it is extremely cold hardy. Its shape makes it very useful as an informal hedge or screen and it is used as a natural snow fence in cold windy regions.

Bright yellow flowers bloom in late spring, with pods forming in late summer. Flowers are like those found on peas, hence the common name pea shrub. Leaves are feathery and young twigs are yellow-green.

Grows best in well-drained sites with full sun or partial shade, but adapts to most soil conditions.

Carissa grandiflora
Natal Plum
Zone: 10. To 2-7 feet.
Evergreen.

Neat shiny leaves, dainty white flowers, and edible fruit make this shrub from South Africa a real asset to the landscape. Low-growing varieties are good ground covers, while taller varieties can be lightly pruned as a tall screen or heavily pruned as a low hedge. They are also used as specimen plants and will grow indoors as houseplants in good light conditions.

Varieties differ in growth habit from loose, open, upright forms to compact spreaders. Most have thorns. The oval leaves are 3 inches long, shiny, and deep green. Fragrant white flowers have 5 petals, are star-shaped, and measure 2 inches across. Blooms year-round. Red, plum-shaped fruits measure 1 to 2 inches around and vary in sweetness.

Natal plums are easy to grow and adapt to a variety of soils. They endure inland's summer heat, or coastal fog, growing both in sun or shade. Fruit quality and quantity will be less if grown in shade. Pruning to remove wild shoots may be needed.

Top-rated varieties include: 'Fancy', upright shrub to 6 feet high; flowers heavily and has large, tasty fruit; 'Green Carpet', a low-grower that reaches 1 to 1-1 2 feet high, spreads to 4 feet, and has small leaves; 'Ruby Point', upright, to 6 feet tall, with beautiful red-tipped foliage year-round.

Natal plums *(Carissa grandiflora)* are evergreen; bear fragrant flowers and bright red, edible fruit year-round. Fruit shown below.

23

Flowering quince *(Chaenomeles sp.)* is striking in early spring when its bright blossoms, shown below, burst open on bare upright branches.

Chaenomeles
Flowering Quince
Zones: 5-9. To 2-10 feet.
Deciduous.

Plants commonly sold as flowering quince are a rather confusing group of species and hybrids in the genus *Chaenomeles.* Even the genus name has been changed from *Pyrus* to *Cydonia* and finally to *Chaenomeles.* Usually nursery plants are labeled simply as flowering quince with a cultivar name. They may be one of several species.

No matter which species you buy, all flowering quince offer brightly colored early spring flowers in shades of white, pink, orange, or red, borne on interestingly twisted, often thorned, bare branches. Flowering quince have a strong Oriental appearance when in full bloom. In fact, cut branches are often used in Oriental flower arrangements.

In the landscape flowering quince can be used as hedges, screens, or as colorful accent plants. Varieties vary from 2 feet to 10 feet high.

They are widely adapted, though they bloom best in areas subject to frequent winter frosts or prolonged cold weather. Plants tolerate a wide range of soil types and temperature extremes.

Convolvulus cneorum
Bush Morning-Glory
Zones: 7-10. To 4 feet.
Evergreen.

Native to southern Europe, bush morning-glory is a rapid-growing, evergreen shrub that grows as wide as it is tall. Leaves are very smooth, silvery-gray, and oval, measuring 2 inches long. Flowers are white or pinkish, with yellow throats. While the flowers are only about 1/2 inch across they are valued for their persistence, blooming from late spring to early fall.

Plant in full sun and well-drained soil. Excellent used in a rock garden, or as a bank cover. Some pruning

may be required because of rapid growth. If plant becomes too leggy, prune severely. It will soon return to a neat, compact form.

Cytisus
Broom

Broom is a common name that actually refers to many plants in three different genera: *Cytisus*, *Genista*, and *Spartium*. They are often confused and mislabeled, because all have pea-shaped flowers that are often sweetly fragrant. The erect branches of broom were cut and used to make brooms, centuries ago, accounting for their common name. Brooms are vigorous plants with a tendency to spread into areas where they are not wanted.

Some *Cytisus* species are evergreen, others are deciduous. However, the distinction makes little difference, since most have bright green stems that have an evergreen appearance whether they have leaves on them or not.

Brooms are easy to grow in well-drained soils, tolerating hot sun, wind, and seashore conditions. Nitrogen-fixing bacteria on the roots make broom adaptable to infertile soils. For best appearance, water occasionally. Too moist or rich soils will cause rank growth and reduced flowering. Lightly prune after flowering to maintain form and remove seed pods.

Cytisus x praecox
Warminster Broom
Zones: 6-9. To 3-5 feet.
Deciduous.

A real showstopper in early spring when covered with light yellow blossoms. Dense green stems give an evergreen effect in winter. Useful as an unpruned hedge or screen.

Cytisus racemosus (Genista racemosa)
Broom
Zones: 7-10. To 6-8 feet.
Evergreen.

This broom is drought-tolerant, making it an excellent shrub for a rocky slope, a dry shrub border, or a sunny rock garden. Many-branched, upright-growing, spreads nearly as wide as tall. Green stems hold silky, evergreen leaflets. In late spring, fragrant, pealike flowers appear in loose terminal sprays, providing a bright, sunny show.

Cytisus scoparius
Scotch Broom
Zones: 6-9. To 10 feet.
Evergreen.

This broom is familar in the Pacific Northwest where it has naturalized with tenacious vigor. Its golden-yellow flowers grace slopes, hill-sides, and open lots in spring and early summer.

A number of varieties that behave better than the species have been developed. 'Andreanus' has blossoms colored burnt red and yellow. 'Burkwoodii' has reddish-rose flowers. 'California' has rose-colored flowers touched with white. 'San Francisco' and 'Stanford' have red blooms. 'Lord Lambourne' has crimson-and-cream flowers. These varieties grow slightly lower, and are more compact than the species. Use for screens, shrub borders, or on slopes.

Daphne odora
Winter Daphne
Zones: 8-10. To 4-6 feet.
Evergreen.

Of all the daphnes, and there are about 50 species, this is the most unforgettable. Its alluring, sweet scent fills the air in early spring. Deep rose to light pink blossoms are borne at the ends of branches in small rounded clusters. A handsome shrub with glossy, 3-inch-long leaves and a compact, upright habit, growing slowly to 4 to 6 feet. It makes a desirable specimen in partly shaded gardens, and is a good low plant for a border, foundation, or accent.

Needs an aerated, well-drained soil to prevent root-rot. Prepare planting hole with ample soil amendments for increased aeration. Plant high to avoid standing

Warminster broom *(Cytisus x praecox)* makes an effective low screen. It bears masses of light yellow flowers in early spring.

Cytisus racemosus, a drought-tolerant broom, is a good choice for rock gardens. It bears fragrant pealike yellow flowers in late spring.

Enkianthus *(Enkianthus campanulatus)* grows tall and upright. Bell-like flowers, shown below, are borne in midspring.

Spring heath *(Erica carnea)* makes a colorful, fine-textured ground cover. Blooms in late winter or early spring.

water around the crown. Avoid fertilizers that will over-acidify soil, but adjust alkaline soils to a more neutral pH. Water sparingly during summer months. Keep roots barely damp and covered with mulch, for a cool soil. Needs pruning very infrequently and has few pest problems, making this lovely plant easy to care for. Mature plants are unpredictable and may die for no apparent reason.

'Marginata', a somewhat hardier form, has yellow-edged leaves. 'Rubra' has deep red flowers, and 'Alba' bears pure white blossoms.

Enkianthus campanulatus

Enkianthus

Zones: 5-9. To 15-20 feet.
Deciduous.

Enkianthus bears clusters of small bell-shaped flowers in midspring that are yellow marked with red. The plant has an interesting layered branching pattern with leaves arranged in whorls. The foliage turns vivid red in fall.

Enkianthus grows best in light shade and moist, well-drained acid soil rich in organic matter. Makes a fine specimen shrub for entryway or patio use.

Erica

Heath

The heaths are a large genus of plants closely related to Scotch heather, *Calluna vulgaris*. They share a need for acid soils, have small scalelike or needlelike leaves, and tiny tubular, bell-shaped flowers borne in late winter to early spring. Heaths are versatile landscape plants with a wide range of growth habits. Some are low-growing ground covers, others are tall and erect, and make excellent hedges and screens.

Erica carnea

Spring Heath

Zones: 4-8. To 6-18 inches.
Evergreen.

This low, spreading plant has up-reaching branches. Leaves are green and needlelike. Rose-colored flowers appear in late winter or early spring depending on climate. Grows best in full sun in cool climates, light shade in hot areas. Trim lightly to keep the plant neat. Makes a colorful ground cover. There are many varieties. 'Ruby Glow' remains small, spreading, and compact, growing to 8 inches; foliage is dark green, flowers deep red. 'Springwood' is also low-growing, with white flowers and light green leaves; an excellent, fast-growing variety. 'Winter Beauty' has pink flowers on a very low plant.

Erica x darleyensis

Darley Heath

Zones: 4-8. To 1-2 feet.
Evergreen.

Winter flowers from November to April make this a most rewarding landscape plant. A hybrid between *E. mediterranea* and *E. carnea,* it is one of the most satisfactory heaths for use as a ground cover. It is also used as a low shrub for foreground plantings, a specimen in rock gardens, or as an edging or dwarf hedge.

Plants in the open will grow 1 foot tall and 3 feet wide. In a closely spaced ground cover planting, can become up to 2 feet tall. Small pink or white urn-shaped flowers in 2-inch-long spikes add a cheery note to the drab winter landscape. The Darley heath is one of the rare heaths and heathers that tolerates alkaline soil.

Escallonia x exoniensis

Escallonia

Zones: 7-10. To 7-10 feet.
Evergreen.

Escallonia is an excellent evergreen shrub with rose-tinted flowers that bloom over a long season from late spring to fall and nearly year-round in warm winter areas. It serves as an attractive screening hedge or windbreak. A fast grower that responds well to trimming, escallonia has small, neat, lustrous green leaves.

Escallonia is a particularly useful shrub in sunny areas near the seashore because it tolerates winds and salt air. Plant in a partly shaded location in hot inland areas. Most soils are suitable for escallonia, except the most alkaline. Partially drought-tolerant, this shrub looks its best if given good drainage and regular watering. Flowering will be reduced by heavy pruning.

'Fradesii' is an excellent compact grower, 5 to 6 feet tall, that flowers prolifically nearly year-round.

Forsythia x intermedia

Border Forsythia

Zones: 5-9. To 9 feet.
Deciduous.

Forsythias are among the earliest blooming deciduous shrubs. In early spring they clothe their bare branches with beautiful clear yellow blossoms. Plants are upright-growing, developing arching canes. They have a spread of 10 to 12 feet, and make handsome specimen plants. They are widely used as a clipped or unclipped hedge, in shrub borders, and in mass or group plantings. Forsythias tolerate a wide range of conditions and have long lives.

Many cultivars have been selected with qualities superior to the parent. 'Lynwood', or 'Lynwood Gold', is a cultivar of Irish origin. It is upright-growing, spreading as wide as it is tall. Branches are covered with golden-yellow blossoms. 'Spring Glory' was introduced in 1942; flowers are rich yellow, borne on upright or spreading branches. 'Spectabilis' is a fast-growing plant with dense, arching branches covered with large deep yellow flowers. Good as an informal hedge. 'Beatrix Farrand' has large, golden, 2-inch flowers with orange markings on the throat.

Fuchsia

Fuchsia

Fuchsias have long been admired for their fine foliage and elegant flowers that grace the garden from early summer to first frost. Hummingbirds are attracted to the brightly colored blossoms.

Escallonia *(Escallonia x exoniensis* 'Fradesii') is covered with rose-tinted flowers nearly year-round in warm winter areas.

The brilliant yellow blooms of border forsythia *(Forsythia x intermedia)* herald spring in most regions of the country.

Fuchsia *(Fuchsia sp.)* produces its graceful blossoms from early summer to autumn frost.

Gardenias *(Gardenia jasminoides)* have glossy evergreen foliage; bear fragrant flowers for many months.

The basic conditions fuchsias require for healthy growth are: good drainage, a rich, moist soil, humid air, and partial shade. Misting foliage and mulching the soil will help create the cool, moist conditions fuchsias enjoy. Under these conditions, fuchsias have a reduced incidence of disease and insect problems, with an additional reward of lush leaves and abundant flowers. The Gulf Coast and especially coastal California are ideal climates for fuchsias.

Both shrubby and trailing fuchsias have been hybridized to create a vast assortment of flower forms in multiple colors ranging from white to pink, red, and purple.

Fuchsia x hybrida
Common Fuchsia
Zones: 9-10. To 2-12 feet.
Evergreen or deciduous.

This fuchsia has many types of glamorous flowers. They can be single or double, measure less than an inch long to over 4 inches long, and have a narrow and tubular or bulbous and flaring shape. Plants are available in either a trailing form suitable for hanging baskets, or as an upright shrub. Erect types make lovely garden shrubs, container plants for patios, and espaliers. Hang trailing plants where they can be admired up close.

This fuchsia remains evergreen in frost-free regions. Elsewhere it is deciduous, or treated as an annual.

Spray, if necessary, to control insect pests such as whitefly, spider mites, and aphids. In early spring, cut back stems of the previous year's growth leaving 2 buds. Can be tip-pruned when actively growing to encourage dense foliage. Container-grown plants also benefit from yearly root pruning.

Fuchsia magellanica
Hardy Fuchsia
Zones: 6-10. To 3-12 feet.
Evergreen or deciduous.

Hardy fuchsia is a widely adapted shrub displaying an abundance of colorful, slender blossoms with bright red sepals and blue inner petals. In Zones 6 to 8, hardy fuchsia acts like a perennial, with its top dying back at the first hard frost. Growth is renewed each year, keeping the plants about 3 feet tall. Hardy fuchsia remains evergreen where winters are mild, and can reach a height of 8 to 12 feet.

Use hardy fuchsia for a long-blooming accent plant or screening hedge. Provide a well-drained, rich soil and plenty of moisture.

Gardenia jasminoides
Gardenia
Zones: 8-10. To 1-8 feet.
Evergreen.

Gardenias are renowned for the memorable fragrance of their waxy blossoms. The flowers are 1 to 5 inches across, opening snow white fading to cream, and bloom from spring until frost. Dark green, thick, shiny, oval leaves are 2 to 4 inches long and are opposite or in 3's on stems.

Growth habit varies from low and spreading, to upright and open, depending on the variety. Gardenias are suitable for hedges and screens, for specimen and border plants. In the North they are grown as houseplants or in greenhouses.

Gardenias grow best in shade. In cool coastal climates they can take full sun, but generally the warmer the climate, the more shade they need. A well-drained, acid soil with ample organic matter is best. Good growth and flowering require summer warmth, ample water, and frequent light fertilization with an acid fertilizer. Prune to remove straggly branches and old flowers.

'Mystery' has large 4- to 5-inch flowers, borne May to July; relatively open-growing to 6 to 8 feet. 'Radicans' grows 6 to 12 inches tall and 2 to 3 feet wide; it has small leaves, 1-inch flowers in late spring. 'Veitchii' is a compact, upright 3- to 4-1/2-foot plant with many 1-1/2-inch flowers from May to November.

Hamamelis x intermedia

Witch Hazel

Zones: 6-8. To 15-18 feet.
Deciduous.

This plant actually represents a group of hybrid witch hazels that are a pure delight in late winter when their bare branches are covered with delicate, wonderfully fragrant, yellow or coppery flowers. They are the showiest blossoms, though not the most fragrant, of the witch hazel family. Leaves are large and rounded, with a bold texture. The variety 'Jelena' has coppery-colored flowers blended with red and orange and red fall foliage color. It has a more spreading habit than the variety 'Magic Fire', which has similar flowers. There are many yellow-flowered varieties.

Plant witch hazel in full sun or partial shade. Should be watered regularly and grown in soil that is rich in organic matter. Use them where their fragrance can be enjoyed, such as in an entryway or near windows. They can also be used as screens or trained into small trees. Flowers are best displayed against a dark background.

Hebe

Hebe

These evergreen shrubs are popular plants in the mild areas of California and the South. Most are native to New Zealand. They are valued for their neat foliage and their red-to-blue, late-blooming flowers. Closely related to *Veronica*, they are often mislabeled as such.

Hebe grows best in cool climates in full sun, with a moist, but well-drained soil. In warmer climates, plant in partial shade. It is useful in windy coastal areas. Use in borders, as low hedges, or as specimens.

Hebe elliptica
Hebe
Zones: 9-10. To 5-6 feet.
Evergreen.

This densely branched shrub has small, 1-inch, green leaves. Fragrant blue flowers are borne in 1- to 2-inch clusters in summer.

Hebe *(Hebe sp.)* is widely used in mild climates for hedges and specimen plants. *Hebe menziesii* 'Coed' blossoms shown below.

29

Hibiscus *(Hibiscus sp.)* bloom in summer; have a variety of flower forms and colors; serve many landscape uses.

Rose-of-Sharon *(Hibiscus syriacus)* blooms late in summer. Useful as a screen or unpruned hedge.

Hebe menziesii
Hebe
Zones: 9-10. To 5 feet.
Evergreen.

With a more spreading habit than most hebes, this species can be used as a tall ground cover. Has neat, tightly packed, lustrous green foliage and bears white flower clusters in summer.

In addition to the above species, the following hybrids are top-rated: 'Autumn Glory', a tight, mounding plant with a neat habit, to 2 feet high; purplish-blue flowers. 'Coed' has attractive, dark green foliage densely packed on reddish stems, to 3 feet high; bears pinkish-purple flowers. 'Reevesii' has attractive foliage mottled reddish purple and green; purplish-red flowers in summer.

Hibiscus
Hibiscus
A large family of plants containing over 200 species of evergreen and deciduous trees, shrubs, and herbs. Two quite different species are top-rated.

Hibiscus rosa-sinensis
Hibiscus, Chinese Hibiscus, Tropical Hibiscus
Zones: 9-10. To 4-15 feet.
Evergreen.

Chinese hibiscus are beautiful plants with spectacular, vividly colored, tropical-looking flowers that bloom in summer. In mild climates they are versatile landscape plants. In cold climates they can be planted in containers and moved to protected areas, or indoors, in winter.

There are many landscape uses for these plants in frost-free climates. They can be used as screen plants, container plants, espaliers, or specimen shrubs and small trees.

Growth habit varies from dense and compact to loose and open. In tropical areas they can reach 30 feet tall. Glossy, pointed, oval leaves differ in size and texture depending upon the variety. Large flowers, 4 to 8 inches wide, may be single or double with smooth or ruffled petals. Colors range from white to red, and yellow to orange, with many multicolor blends. Many varieties are grown.

Good soil drainage is essential. If your soil does not drain well, plant hibiscus in raised beds or containers. Flowering is best in full sun except in hot inland areas where afternoon shade is preferred. Protect plants from strong winds. Warm temperatures are required for flower production. Water thoroughly and frequently. Fertilize plants monthly from April through August. Container plants need feeding twice a month.

Pinch and remove irregular branches to develop good branch structure on young plants. Remove 1/3 of the old wood on mature plants in early spring to encourage vigorous growth.

Protection from overhanging roofs or evergreen trees helps plants survive light frost. Where the temperature drops below 30°F, grow hibiscus in containers and move to a well-lighted, indoor area for winter.

Hibiscus syriacus
Rose-of-Sharon, Shrub Althaea
Zones: 5-10. To 8-12 feet.
Deciduous.

Rose-of-Sharon is a longtime favorite that has been grown for centuries in Europe and the United States. Two valued characteristics are its late summer blooming season and its adaptability to eastern coastal conditions. The shrub has a tall vase-shape suitable for a screen or unpruned hedge, or a specimen or accent plant.

Leaves are green with toothed margins, sometimes lobed. Flowers come in single, semidouble, and double forms, in white and pink, red, and purple shades. They are usually 2 to 4 inches across. Single-type flowers are the largest. Single flowers and some semidouble flowers are followed by unattractive seed pods. Many varieties are grown.

Plant in full sun or partial shade. Likes heat and will take some drought. Grows best with regular watering. Prune to encourage compact shape. Heavy pruning also encourages larger flower size.

Hydrangea
Hydrangea

This genus includes 23 species of erect or climbing, deciduous or evergreen shrubs native to east Asia, and North and South America. Flowers are borne in clusters and, depending upon the species, may be white, pink, lavender, or blue and appear in mid- or late summer.

A rich, porous, consistently moist, well-drained soil is required. Hydrangeas bloom freely in full sun in cool areas but are best in partial shade, protected from hot afternoon sun. For best flowering, prune to remove old stems, and thin young stems.

Hydrangea arborescens
Smooth Hydrangea, Hills-of-Snow
Zones: 5-9. To 3-5 feet.
Deciduous.

Native to the eastern United States, this species forms a rounded bush and has balls of cream-white flowers in midsummer. Weak stems are often weighed to the ground by the heavy flower heads. The cultivar 'Annabelle' has huge, 10-inch, snow-white flower heads. 'Grandiflora', a common cultivar, is known as hills-of-snow; blooms heavily for several months beginning in early summer.

Hydrangea macrophylla
Big-Leaf Hydrangea
Zones: 6-10. To 6-10 feet.
Deciduous.

This large rounded shrub has bold-textured shiny leaves with toothed edges. Large ball-like flower clusters bloom in mid- and late summer. Soil pH influences flower color. Acid soils produce blue flowers; pink or red blooms result from alkaline soils. If you desire pink flowers, add garden lime to the soil. If blue flowers are desired, add a tablespoon of aluminum sulfate.

Big-leaf hydrangea *(Hydrangea macrophylla)* is bold and dramatic. Flower color can be changed by modifying soil pH. Add aluminum sulfate for blue flowers.

Hills-of-snow *(Hydrangea arborescens),* below left; peegee hydrangea *(Hydrangea paniculata),* below right.

Oakleaf hydrangea blossoms *(Hydrangea quercifolia)* are showy in late spring. Foliage turns red in fall.

Aaron's-beard *(Hypericum calycinum)* thrives in sun or shade. Forms a dense ground cover brightened in summer by sunny yellow flowers, below.

A long list of varieties are available, many of which were developed for greenhouse forcing. 'Tricolor' has foliage variegated with light green and creamy white.

Hydrangea paniculata
**Panicle Hydrangea,
Peegee Hydrangea**
Zones: 5-9. To 20 feet.
Deciduous or evergreen.

This large shrub or small tree can be used as a specimen or hedge plant. It spreads as wide as it is tall. The cultivar 'Grandiflora', the peegee hydrangea, is usually grown. It is a vigorous plant valued for its long-lasting, large, pyramidal clusters of white flowers, which fade to rosy-brown. Blooms after hills-of-snow and big-leaf hydrangea.

Hydrangea quercifolia
Oakleaf Hydrangea
Zones: 6-9. To 6 feet.
Deciduous.

This species has large, attractive lobed leaves to 8 inches long, resembling those of an oak. They turn bronzy-red in fall. Large, cone-shaped clusters of white flowers are showy in late spring. Can be pruned heavily each year to maintain a lower height. Takes a bit more sun than other hydrangeas.

Hypericum
St. John's-Wort

This large genus is comprised primarily of herbaceous perennials, but two forms make top-rated flowering shrubs.

Hypericum calycinum
**Aaron's-Beard,
Creeping St. John's-Wort**
Zones: 5-10. To 12 inches.
Evergreen or semideciduous.

This low, spreading plant is valued as a tenacious ground cover for sun or shade. Green leaves are 4 inches long. Bright yellow flowers measure 3 inches across and are borne throughout the summer. Aaron's-beard will form a dense ground cover in the toughest situations. It spreads by underground stems and is so vigorous it often grows into areas where it is not wanted, unless it is contained.

Space plants 12 to 18 inches apart for a quick cover. Mow to the ground every second or third winter to keep its growth lush.

Hypericum 'Hidcote'
Hidcote Hypericum
Zones: 5-10. To 4 feet.
Evergreen.

This shrubby hypericum is useful as a hedge or for massed plantings. Has an arching shape. It is semideciduous in cold winter areas, and may be partially killed to the ground in northern extremes of its growing region, remaining about 2 feet high. Leaves have a blue-green tint. Yellow flowers, 3 inches across, are borne throughout the summer.

Kolkwitzia amabilis
Beautybush
Zones: 5-8. To 7-8 feet.
Deciduous.

This upright shrub bears arching or pendulous branches that bend to the ground. Small light pink flowers with yellow throats cover the branches in early spring. Trunk and twigs have attractive peeling bark.

Grows well in dry, poor soil and in sun or shade. Relatively free of insect and disease problems. Do not prune—allow branches to cascade. Use as a specimen plant or as a screen.

Lagerstroemia indica
Crape Myrtle
Zones: 7-9. To 5-15 feet.
Deciduous.

The profusion of colorful flowers that appear from summer to fall makes this a useful landscape plant. Normally grown as a small tree, shrub-types good for foundation plantings, shrub borders, and hedges have been developed. Shrub-types will grow and bloom in the warmest parts of Zone 6 if the roots are protected with a mulch.

They can then be treated as perennials, because flowers are formed on new growth that will sprout from the roots. Tree-types can be kept low with pruning.

The glossy, dark green leaves are 1/2 inch long and 3/4 to 1-1/4 inches wide. Fall color depends on the climate and variety but leaves can turn yellow, orange, or brilliant red. Clusters of ruffled flowers, 6 to 15 inches tall, are crinkled like crepe paper and open from July to September. Individual flowers are up to 1-1/2 inches across and have 5 to 8 petals. Colors are white, pink, rose, red, lavender, and purple. Crape myrtles also have smooth, interestingly mottled gray or light brown bark.

Many selections are available trained in tree or shrub forms. The 'Petite' series is shrubby, with plants growing 5 to 7 feet tall in a full color range. 'Crape Myrtlettes', an even smaller-growing group, is raised from seed.

Mildew can be a serious problem in humid or cool areas. It can be controlled by fungicides. A group of mildew-tolerant varieties, bearing the names of Indian tribes, has been developed at the U.S. National Arboretum. Varieties in different flower colors and with colorful bark are available.

Lantana

Lantana

There are over 155 species of lantana native to North and South America and parts of Europe. They are sun-loving plants highly valued for their abundant flowers that bloom for many months of the year. In frost-free areas plants remain evergreen. In colder climates they can be treated as annuals or half-hardy perennials. These fast-growing shrubs tolerate heat, drought, and poor soils, making them problem-solvers in many tough landscape situations. Lantanas make a colorful display draped over a raised planter, in a hanging basket, or used on a bank to help stabilize soil. Shrub-types can

Lantana *(Lantana sp.)* is an easy-care shrub adapted to difficult sites in mild climates.

Beautybush *(Kolkwitzia amabilis)*

33

Bush lantana *(Lantana camara)* forms a colorful carpet of blossoms from spring to late fall. Yellow flowers turn red with age.

Bell-shaped white flowers adorn drooping leucothoe *(Leucothoe fontanesiana)* in spring. Hardy, thrives in shade.

be used as a low hedge or in foundation plantings.

Lantanas are easy-care shrubs, requiring a minimum of watering and fertilizing. Occasional heavy pruning in early spring or fall will help keep the plant neat and free of woody growth. Watch for signs of mealybugs and whiteflies.

Numerous hybrids between the two common species of lantana are available, offering a wide selection of flower colors and plant forms.

Lantana camara
Bush Lantana
Zones: 9-10. To 4-6 feet. Evergreen.

This robust shrub has pungent, prickly leaves. Flowers appear from spring to late fall, or year-round where winter weather stays warm. Flat-topped, 2-inch flower clusters cover the plant with yellow blossoms that become red as they age.

Lantana montevidensis (L. sellowiana)
Trailing Lantana
Zones: 9-10. To 1 foot. Evergreen.

Decorated most of the year with a profusion of lavender flowers, trailing lantana is a low-growing shrub with weak stems that spread 3 feet or more.

Leucothoe fontanesiana
Drooping Leucothoe
Zones: 5-8. To 2-6 feet. Evergreen.

This slow-growing relative of lily-of-the-valley shrub *(Pieris sp.)* is native to the eastern United States. Glossy, dark green leaves 4 to 7 inches long have a purplish cast in winter. Creamy-white, drooping clusters of bell-shaped flowers are borne in spring. Varieties available include 'Rainbow' with green leaves marked with creamy-yellow.

Grows best in a shady, moist site with acid soil. Spreads by underground stems. Attractive in massed plantings. Prune to control size.

Lonicera tatarica
Tatarian Honeysuckle
Zones: 3-9. To 8-10 feet. Deciduous.

This is one of the hardiest and most reliable flowering shrubs for cold climates. Forms a many-branched, dense shrub with deep green leaves. Small, pinkish, very fragrant flowers appear in late spring and early summer and are followed by yellow or red berries. Makes an effective screen or informal hedge. Grows in most soils and is pest-free. Grow in full sun or partial shade.

'Alba' is a white-flowering form. 'Rosea' has pink flowers with deeper colored outsides. *Zabelii* has dark red flowers.

Magnolia
Magnolia
Zones: 5-10. Deciduous.

Magnolia species are generally grown as multi-stemmed trees, however when *Magnolia x soulangiana* and *Magnolia stellata* are pruned to control size, they make excellent spring-blooming shrubs. Complete descriptions of these two species are in the book *Top-Rated Flowering Trees.*

Mahonia
Mahonia

These evergreen shrubs with shiny, spiny-margined, compound leaves are related to barberries and are sometimes labeled as species of *Berberis*. They are also sometimes mistaken for hollies. They produce clusters or spikes of yellow flowers in spring that are followed by blue-black berries, which are relished by birds. Use the taller species for textural contrast in a shrub border and use lower-growing species as ground covers or barrier plants.

Mahonia aquifolium
Oregon Grape
Zones: 5-9. To 2-6 feet.
Evergreen.

Oregon grape forms a large stand of upright stems that grow from spreading, underground stems. Native to the Pacific Northwest, it makes a good plant wherever masses of low, evergreen foliage are needed. Leaves are 4 to 10 inches long with 5 to 9 spiny-margined, oval leaflets that are 1 to 2-1/2 inches long. The upper surface is glossy or dull depending upon the variety. New growth is often coppery. Winter foliage turns maroon, especially in areas where winters are cold. 'Compacta' makes a tidy, uniform, 2-foot-high mound.

Grows in sun or shade in cool areas. Best in shade in warm areas. Tolerates acid or slightly alkaline soils. Height can be controlled by pruning. Prune to the ground to thicken the stand.

Mahonia bealei
Leatherleaf Mahonia
Zones: 5-10. To 10-12 feet.
Evergreen.

A native to China, this bold-textured plant with strong vertical stems makes a striking contrast to less dramatic plants. The 12- to 16-inch-long leathery leaves are made up of 7 to 15 leaflets that are 2 to 4-1/2 inches long and have 2 to 5 large spines on each margin. The upper leaf surfaces are dull, bluish green, and the undersides are gray-green.

Leatherleaf mahonia is a shade plant except in cool coastal areas where it can be grown in full sun. Soil should be moist and contain plenty of organic matter.

Mahonia lomariifolia
Chinese Holly-Grape
Zones: 8-10. To 6-10 feet.
Evergreen.

The long, deeply divided, dark green leaves of this *Mahonia* are arranged horizontally around upright

Tatarian honeysuckle *(Lonicera tatarica)* has fragrant flowers, bright berries. Cold hardy. Makes a good screen or hedge.

Oregon grape *(Mahonia aquifolium)*

35

Heavenly bamboo *(Nandina domestica)* lends an open airy feeling and changing foliage color to the landscape.

Oleanders *(Nerium oleander)* are drought-tolerant; widely used for screens, hedges, and specimen plants in mild climates.

stems and may be more than 2 feet long. Leaf margins are spiny. Yellow flowers in clusters to 6 inches long appear in late winter or early spring and are followed by powder-blue berries.

Chinese holly-grape makes an excellent accent plant for entryways, patios, or container growing. Its bold texture is best set off by a fine-textured ground cover. Grow in partial shade. Prune branch tips to encourage branching.

Nandina domestica

Heavenly Bamboo

Zones: 6-10. To 3-8 feet.
Evergreen or semideciduous.

Heavenly bamboo has slender, vertical stems decorated with dark green, delicate foliage that suggests bamboo, although they are not related. It is often used to create an Oriental feeling in gardens where bamboo can't be grown. New leaves are tinted a bronzy-pink, later soft green, and change to dramatic shades of crimson and purple in the winter. Large white flower clusters appear in July followed by brilliant red berries that last for several months.

Heavenly bamboo is considered one of the most versatile shrubs for sun or shade, suitable for using in narrow spaces, containers, borders, and for foundation plantings. Plant shrubs in groupings for cross-pollination and more berry production.

Roots compete well in crowded conditions in almost any soil, although plants become somewhat chlorotic in alkaline conditions. Resistant to oak root fungus and free of pests, heavenly bamboo is fairly drought-tolerant once established. In areas where temperatures reach below 0°F, treat it as an herbaceous perennial. Leaves are deciduous at 10°F. Remove all weak shoots to increase density. Prune tops to reduce height. 'Alba' is a white-berried variety. 'Nana' grows to only 12 to 18 inches high. 'Compacta' is also restrained, but reaches 4 to 5 feet.

Nerium oleander

Oleander

Zones: 8-10. To 8-20 feet.
Evergreen.

Oleander has one of the longest flowering seasons of any shrub, blooming from May or June until September. Plants usually develop a broad, bulky form at a moderate to fast rate, and are often used for hedges and screens. A small single- or multiple-trunked tree, with branches starting at 7 or 8 feet, can be developed by pruning.

Thick, glossy dark green leaves 3 to 6 inches long and 3/4 to 1 inch wide are usually arranged in whorls of three. Forms with leaves to 12 inches long, and gold-variegated leaves are sometimes available. Flaring, waxy flowers measuring 1-1/2 to 3 inches wide are borne in clusters at twig or branch tips. Varieties with single or double flowers in white, yellow, salmon, pink, and red are available. Some varieties have fragrant blooms.

Oleanders are not particular about soil and withstand considerable drought, poor drainage, and relatively high soil salt levels. They also take heat and strong light, including reflected heat from paving, and tolerate wind, air pollution, and salt spray. They are very adaptable and flourish in hot, dry interior areas as well as in coastal locations. Growth is best in full sun in moist, well-drained soil.

All parts of oleander are poisonous to people and livestock. Don't use the wood for barbeque skewers. Also, smoke from burning plant parts can cause severe irritation.

Philadelphus

Mock Orange

Mock oranges are admired for their perfumed white flowers that have the sweet fragrance of orange blossoms. They bloom in late spring or early summer, after the majority of spring-flowering shrubs have faded, making them valuable landscape plants. Shrubs are vase-shaped with spreading or drooping branches.

Mock oranges are tough, durable plants, and although not too particular, grow best in a well-drained, loamy soil with lots of organic matter. They are easily grown, with few problems, if located in full sun or light shade. Partial shade is required in the hottest areas. Prune after flowering if necessary. Blossoms are produced on 1-year-old wood.

Mock oranges are used as specimen plants, in mass plantings, and in shrub borders. Lower-growing types make useful hedges or dividers.

Philadelphus coronarius
Sweet Mock Orange
Zones: 5-8. To 12 feet.
Deciduous.

This old-fashioned plant has been brightening gardens for centuries. It should have intensely sweet-scented flowers, but inferior plants are sometimes sold. Purchase blooming plants with good fragrance. It tends to become leggy in confined spaces or when planted too close to buildings, so give it room to develop. Will grow as wide as it is tall. The cultivar 'Nanus' grows to 4 feet high.

Philadelphus x lemoinei
Lemoine Mock Orange
Zones: 5-8. To 5-6 feet.
Deciduous.

This hybrid mock orange has very fragrant flowers to 1-1/2 inches across. The cultivar 'Enchantment' has erect branches with free-flowering, double, white blossoms that are only lightly fragrant. 'Innocence', growing to 8 feet tall, has wonderfully fragrant flowers, 1 to 2 inches across.

Philadelphus x virginalis
Virginalis Mock Orange
Zones: 4-8. To 6-8 feet.
Deciduous.

Produces masses of large, semidouble, fragrant white blooms that are often used for cut flowers. Fast-growing, this mock orange likes

Mock orange *(Philadelphus sp.)* is a durable plant bearing orange-blossom-scented white flowers. Double-flowered form shown below.

Red-tip photinia *(Photinia x fraseri)* has red foliage year-round. New leaves are bronzy-red; white flowers in spring, shown below, are followed by red berries.

Lily-of-the-valley shrub *(Pieris japonica)* is widely grown for its evergreen foliage and early spring bloom.

full sun and open situations. Tolerates coastal conditions in the eastern United States. The cultivar 'Virginal' blooms all summer and has 2-inch, semidouble, white flowers. 'Minnesota Snowflake' has large, double, fragrant flowers and is hardy to −30°F.

Photinia x fraseri

Red-Tip Photinia

Zones: 7-10. To 10-12 feet.
Evergreen.

The bright, bronzy-red new leaves of photinia can equal any flowering shrub for a colorful display in early spring. Large, flat-headed clusters of white flowers follow in March and April, with subsequent red berries, which attract birds, continuing to add visual interest. The lustrous, heat-tolerant foliage is useful as an attractive background for other plants. Photinia is a large-scale screening shrub growing moderately fast to 10 feet high and spreading somewhat wider. It responds well to pruning for a neat shape or formal hedge. Young plants may be trained as attractive small trees.

Photinia readily accepts high heat and sun if watered regularly, or drier conditions in partial shade. Provide a well-drained soil rich in organic matter. Aphids and scale are occasional problems. Photinia is also susceptible to fireblight.

Pieris

Pieris, Andromeda

This genus contains 8 species of evergreen shrubs or small trees. These are ornamental plants grown for their foliage and clusters of white or pink flowers in spring. A moist, acid, well-drained soil, with high organic content is required. Will grow in sun or partial shade but dislikes strong winds. Responds well to frequent light applications of acid fertilizers.

Pieris floribunda

Fetterbush, Mountain Andromeda
Zones: 5-9. To 6 feet.
Evergreen.

This dense shrub is native to the Southeastern United States, Virginia to Georgia. It is the hardiest of the *Pieris*. Bears upright pyramidal clusters of white flowers in early spring.

'Karenoma' is a fast-growing compact shrub with snow-white flowers in early spring.

Pieris japonica

Andromeda, Japanese Pieris, Lily-of-the-Valley Shrub
Zones: 5-9. To 9-10 feet.
Evergreen.

Dangling clusters of tiny flower buds decorate this broad-leaved evergreen all winter. In very early spring, they open to snowy-white, occasionally pale pink, flowers that resemble lily-of-the-valley blossoms.

Many cultivars are available. 'Valley Rose' is one of the newer cultivars with pink flowers; grows 4 to 6 feet tall. 'Red Mill' has bright red new growth; grows to 12 feet tall. 'Variegata' has green leaves edged with white; forms a compact dense shrub 5 to 7 feet tall. 'Flamingo' has pink flowers; tall-growing, can reach 10 feet. 'Mountain Fire' is a heavy bloomer with white flowers; new spring foliage is bright red; grows to 10 feet in height.

Pittosporum tobira

Tobira, Mock Orange

Zones: 8-10. To 6-15 feet.
Evergreen.

Lustrous leaves, fragrant flowers, and low maintenance are responsible for the popularity of tobira. It is a good foundation, specimen, or screening plant. It grows well in containers, and in cold areas can be protected during the winter.

This medium-sized shrub grows vigorously and has a broad, upright shape and heavy branches. The leathery, glossy, dark green leaves are 1-1/2 to 4 inches long and 3/4 to 1-1/2 inches wide, with rounded ends and a pale midrib and are spaced so closely together that the plant has a very solid appearance. Creamy-white, five-petaled flowers have the scent of orange blossoms, accounting for the common name mock orange. They are about 1 inch across and are produced in 2- to 3-inch clusters at the branch tips in spring. Petals yellow with age. Small pear-shaped seed capsules split in fall revealing orange seeds.

Plant in sun or semishade. Fairly drought-resistant, but appearance is enhanced with moderate watering. Feed once a year in spring with a nitrogen fertilizer to produce greener, larger leaves. Not as tolerant to shearing as some other pittosporums. Head back and thin out to control growth. Aphids and scale are major insect problems.

'Variegata' has attractive gray-green leaves, edged with white; reaches an ultimate height of only 5 feet. 'Wheeler's Dwarf' is a 1- to 2-foot, mounding plant with dense, whorled foliage; fragrant flowers are the same as on the larger-growing type; good foreground, border, or hedge plant.

Potentilla fruticosa
Shrubby Cinquefoil
Zones: 2-9. To 4 feet.
Deciduous.

This many-branched, spreading shrub produces large numbers of bright yellow flowers throughout the summer, making it a prized garden shrub. Native from Labrador to Alaska, where it survives temperatures to −50°F, shrubby cinquefoil is also native in the Rocky Mountains to elevations over 11,000 feet and to Europe and Asia.

Shrubby cinquefoil withstands heat, drought, and poor soils. Best growth and fuller, more abundant bloom is produced on plants growing in moist but well-drained soils in full sunlight. Plants on excessively dry sites grow more slowly.

Tobira *(Pittsoporum tobira)* is a fine foundation, specimen, or screening plant. White flowers in spring have the fragrance of orange blossoms.

Shrubby cinquefoil *(Potentilla fruticosa)* shown below, withstands heat, cold and drought. Bountiful yellow flowers appear in summer.

English laurel (*Prunus laurocerasus*) makes an excellent hedge.

Carolina cherry laurel (*Prunus caroliniana*)

Many cultivars have been developed for garden use, with new forms being offered almost every year. Popular varieties include: 'Abbotswood' with white flowers; 'Katherine Dykes' with early yellow blossoms; 'Klondike', low-growing, with yellow blooms; 'Moonlight' with yellowish-white flowers; 'Mount Everest' with white flowers; and 'Red Ace', a profusely blooming variety, with red flowers.

Prunus

Flowering Fruit, Prunus

Several species of this large genus noted for its ornamental flowers and delicious fruits are top-rated flowering shrubs.

Prunus caroliniana
Carolina Cherry Laurel
Zones: 7-10. To 20-40 feet.
Evergreen.

A large evergreen shrub or small tree, this species makes an effective large screen or clipped hedge in warm climates such as its native North Carolina to Texas region.

Growth rate is moderate to rapid. Leaves are deep glossy green, 2 to 4 inches long, and have smooth edges. Foliage is bronze-colored when young. Small, cream-white flowers in 1-inch spikes open between February and April. Black fruits, 1/2 inch or less in diameter, last into winter if birds don't eat them. Falling fruit can be messy.

The variety 'Compacta' is slow-growing and compact. 'Bright 'n Tight' is also small and compact. Both make excellent hedges.

Cherry laurel grows well in average soil but shows chlorosis and leaf burn in alkaline soils. Growth is best in cool, moist coastal areas but shrubs can take full sun and high heat. Established plants are drought-tolerant.

Prunus x cistena
Purple-Leaf Sand Cherry, Dwarf Red-Leaf Plum
Zones: 2-9. To 6-8 feet.
Deciduous.

These are very valuable plants in the coldest regions. White or pink spring flowers are followed by black fruit. Attractive leaves are purplish all summer. Grow in full sun and well-drained soil.

Prunus laurocerasus
English Laurel
Zones: 7-10. To 5-30 feet.
Evergreen.

This rapid-growing shrub can easily reach 30 feet tall and as wide in mild climates. In cold areas growth will be curtailed. Makes a very effective screen or clipped hedge although the fast growth calls for frequent clipping. Glossy dark green, oval leaves are 3 to 7 inches long. Small, fragrant white flowers stand above the foliage in long clusters. They are followed by small black fruits. Has invasive roots.

Takes full sun in cool climates. Grow in partial shade in hot areas. 'Otto Luyken' is a low-growing variety.

Pyracantha
Firethorn

Six species of evergreen, usually thorny, shrubs of this genus native to southeastern Europe and Asia are grown as ornamentals. They are used as specimen plants, in barrier hedges, and as espaliers. When trained as espaliers they can grow twice the height they achieve as a shrub. Some forms can be pruned into single-stemmed small trees.

Flat clusters of petite white flowers make a pretty display in spring. The real color show begins in late summer or early autumn when the large clusters of berries turn red to orange. They persist into winter.

Firethorns thrive in a wide variety of well-drained soils. A sunny location is preferred. Although most species are evergreen, leaves may be winter-killed in cold northern climates.

In some areas some pyracantha varieties are subject to fireblight, a disease that kills branches. They can also be susceptible to apple scab, which blackens fruit and can defoliate the shrub. Select one of the recently developed disease-resistant hybrids such as: 'Fiery Cascade', which grows to 8 feet tall; 'Mohave', which grows to 12 feet tall; 'Rutgers', which grows to 3 feet tall and spreads to 9 feet; and 'Teton', which reaches 15 feet high. All are adapted to Zones 6 to 9.

Pyracantha angustifolia
Narrowleaf Firethorn
Zones: 5-9. To 12 feet.
Evergreen.

Though this species usually grows upright, prostrate forms are available. Narrow leaves measure 2 inches long. White flowers are in clusters 1-1/2 inches wide. The bright orange to brick-red berries are highly ornamental and are retained through winter.

The cultivar 'Gnome' is hardier and grows half as tall as the species with a compact, densely branched growth habit. Masses of orange berries are borne in late summer or early fall.

Pyracantha coccinea
Scarlet Firethorn
Zones: 5-9. To 6 feet.
Deciduous or evergreen.

This species is popular because of its masses of bright red fruits that appear in autumn. Leaves drop during winter in colder regions.

While the species, hardy only to Zone 7, is rarely grown, many superior cultivars are available. 'Lalandei' is hardier than the species, growing into Zone 5. Grows vigorously to 10 feet. Orange-red fruits are borne during fall. It is resistant to fireblight. 'Kasan' is also hardier than the species and is one of the most cold-tolerant of all scarlet firethorn cultivars. Bright orange-red fruits are held well into the winter. 'Colorado Red', a vigorous-growing plant with bright red berries, is hardy into Zone 5.

Firethorn *(Pyracantha sp.)* is admired for its clusters of spring flowers and brilliant display of long-lasting berries, shown below.

A shrub for all seasons, Indian hawthorn *(Raphiolepis sp.)* blooms from midwinter through spring, again in fall; bears blue-black berries. New foliage, shown below, is often bronzy-red, turns to deep green.

Pyracantha koidzumii
Formosa Firethorn
Zones: 7-10. To 10 feet.

This densely branched shrub bears abundant small orange-red to dark red berries and spreads to 8 feet. 'Santa Cruz Prostrata' is a creeping variety with masses of red berries borne in autumn.

Pyracantha 'Tiny Tim'
Tiny Tim Firethorn
Zones: 7-9. To 3 feet.

This dwarf is nearly thornless, with cinnamon-red fruits. Used in borders, foundations, or patio planters.

Raphiolepis indica
Indian Hawthorn
Zones: 8-10. To 2-5 feet.
Evergreen.

Neat evergreen foliage, pretty blossoms, and colorful berries give Indian hawthorn a top-rated reputation as a ground cover, informal hedge, colorful accent, and a foundation shrub. Its restrained growth and heat tolerance also make it useful for growing in large containers or raised planters.

Handsome, leathery foliage is often bronzy or red when young, changing to deep green. From midwinter through spring, and again in fall, a profusion of flowers appears. Varieties are available with white, pink, or deep rose-red blossoms, in growth forms from low and compact to tall and upright. Bluish-black berries are held through winter.

Indian hawthorn is adaptable to a wide range of soils. Fairly drought-tolerant, it does best with regular watering. In full sun, it will bloom prolifically but is quite suitable for partly shaded locations. Pinch back growing tips after flowering for dense, sturdy shrubs, or thin occasionally for a more open form. Leaf spot, aphids, and fireblight are occasional problems.

The variety 'Apple Blossom' has white-and-pink blossoms. 'Bill Evans' grows quickly to 5 to 7 feet, and has pink flowers and heavy-textured foliage. 'Coates Crimson' has crimson-pink flowers on a 2- to 4-foot plant. 'Rosea Dwarf' has a dense, compact habit from 2 to 4 feet high with light pink flowers. 'Snow White' bears white flowers on a 4-foot plant.

Rhododendron
Rhododendron, Azalea

There are over 900 species and more than 10,000 named varieties in the genus *Rhododendron*, which includes all the plants once placed in the genus *Azalea*. They are native to many parts of the world including North America. Plants range from large trees to low-growing shrubs only a few inches high. Flowers are borne in clusters or singly, and individual blossoms are single, semidouble, double, or hose-in-hose. Double blossoms result from stamens becoming petal-like. Hose-in-hose flowers are formed when the sepals (the green "leaves" at the bases of the flowers) become petallike. Hose-in-hose flowers may be single, double, or semidouble. Leaves vary from large and leathery to small and fine-textured. Plants may be either evergreen or deciduous.

Most people think of azaleas as low-growing, compact plants that cover themselves with bright-colored blossoms in late winter or early spring. Rhododendrons are thought of as taller plants with heavier foliage and large clusters of blossoms. Botanists have found the distinctions a bit more complex but for a gardener's purpose those distinctions are adequate.

Complete descriptions of rhododendron and azalea varieties and species can be found in *Top-Rated Azaleas and Rhododendrons*, another book in this series.

Azalea

Botanists have organized the genus *Rhododendron* into series and sub-series and azaleas are one of the prime series. Azaleas are further categorized into the following groups of hybrids with special characteristics; each group has its own named varieties in a wide range of flower types and colors. The evergreen varieties are listed first, in order of least to most cold hardy, followed by the deciduous kinds.

Evergreen Azaleas

Belgian Indica: Evergreen. Developed for greenhouse forcing, these plants have become popular for landscape use in mild climates. They have lush foliage and produce copious quantities of large double or semidouble flowers. Hardy to 20° to 30°F, Zones 8-10.

Rutherfordiana: Evergreen. Originally developed for greenhouse forcing, they are attractive, small bushy plants with handsome foliage and abundant single, semidouble, or double blossoms of medium size. Hardy to 20° to 30°F, Zones 8-10.

Southern Indica: Evergreen. Tough, outdoor versions of the Belgian Indicas. Grow more vigorously and taller than Belgians. They are able to take full sun. Profuse small to medium-sized single blossoms are borne in midspring. Hardy to 20°F, Zones 8-10.

Satsuki: Evergreen. Late blooming. Will grow in full sun. Good to extend the flowering season of azaleas. Hardy 5° to 10°F, Zones 7-10.

Kurume: Evergreen. These familiar azaleas of Japan are compact with dense small leaves and masses of small flowers. Branches often layered in tiers. Will grow in half a day of sun. Hardy to 5° to 10°F, Zones 7-10.

Macrantha: Evergreen. Late blooming, compact plants with larger flowers than Kurumes. Hardy to 5°F, Zones 7-10.

Pericat: Evergreen. Developed for greenhouse forcing, these hybrids of Belgian Indicas and Kurumes greatly resemble Kurumes but have larger flowers. Hardy to 5° to 10°F, Zones 7-10.

Evergreen azaleas *(Rhododendron sp.)* make a handsome informal border year-round that is spectacular during spring when in flower.

'Hershey Red' (above left) and 'Coral Bells' (above right) are both evergreen Kurume azaleas *(Rhododendron sp.)*.

43

Azaleas *(Rhododendron sp.)* are widely used as colorful container plants.

Exbury hybrid azaleas *(Rhododendron sp.)* bear masses of squarish blossoms speckled with contrasting colors.

Gable Hybrids: Evergreen but may drop leaves in cold climates. Cold-hardy version of Kurume hybrids. Compact plants with heavy bloom in midspring. Many varieties have medium-sized hose-in-hose blossom. Hardy to 0°F, Zones 6-8.

Glenn Dale Hybrids: Evergreen. Bred primarily for cold hardiness. Group includes a wide variety of flower types and sizes. May loose a few leaves in cold winters. Grows best in half-sun. Hardy to 0° to 10°F, Zones 7-9.

Kaempferi Hybrids: Evergreen. Hardier than Kurumes, with a tall, upright habit and flowers including a color range of orange and red. Slightly larger than Kurumes. Hardy to −15°F, Zones 5-9.

Deciduous Azaleas

Knap Hill and Exbury Hybrids: Deciduous. These large-flowered hybrids were bred in England by the Knap Hill Nursery at the Rothschild's estate in Exbury, England. Clusters of squarish often fragrant flowers. Colors include cream, yellow, orange, pink, and red. Grows to 5 feet tall. Hardy to −20°F, Zones 5-8.

Mollis Hybrids: Deciduous. Clusters of red, orange, or yellow flowers. Grows 4 or 5 feet tall. Hardy to −20°F, Zones 5-8.

Occidentale Hybrids: Deciduous. Flowers in clusters are colored white with a pink tinge, or yellow and red with orange markings. Grows to 8 feet tall. Hardy to −5°F, Zones 6-8.

Ghent Hybrids: Deciduous. Flowers red, yellow, or pink, smaller than those of Mollis hybrids. Grows 4 to 6 feet tall. Very cold hardy to −25°F, Zones 4-8.

Rhododendrons

Rhododendrons are among the most important flowering shrubs in northern gardens. Many take sub-zero winters in stride, then cover themselves with magnificent flowers in spring.

The following rhododendrons are the most popular according to a recent poll of 20 chapters of the American Rhododendron Society, located in many different geographic regions.

The ARS rating included in the description of each of the following plants is a measure of quality. The first number refers to flower quality and the second to shrub quality. An "ideal" rating is 5/5. Also included in each description are the minimum temperature tolerated, plant height, flower color, and time of bloom. The flowering season varies depending on the growing region. In general, "early" is April, "mid-season" is May, and "late" is late May or June.

'Anah Kruschke': −10°F. ARS rating 2/3. 6 feet. Flowers lavender-blue to reddish purple. Late.

'Anna Rose Whitney': −5°F. ARS rating 3/3. 6 feet. Flowers large, rose-pink. Mid- to late season.

'Antoon van Welie': −5°F. ARS rating 3/3. 6 feet. Flowers deep pink. Mid- to late season.

'Boule de Neige': −25°F. ARS rating 4/4. 5 feet. Flowers white. Mid-season.

'Bow Bells': 0°F. ARS rating 3/4. 3 feet. Flowers light pink. Early to midseason.

'Caroline': −15°F. ARS rating 3/3. 6 feet. Flowers orchid-pink. Mid- to late season.

'Dora Amateis': −15°F. ARS rating 4/4. 3 feet. Flowers pure white. Early to midseason.

'Fragrantissimum': 20°F. ARS rating 4/3. 5 feet. Flowers white tinged pink. Fragrant. Midseason.

'Janet Blair': −15°F. ARS rating 4/3. 6 feet. Flowers light pink. Mid- to late season.

'The Hon. Jean Marie de Montague': 0°F. ARS rating 3/4. 5 feet. Flowers bright red. Midseason.

'Mrs. Furnival': −10°F. ARS rating 5/5. 4 feet. Flowers light pink. Mid- to late season.

'Nova Zembla': −25°F. ARS rating 3/3. 5 feet. Flowers dark red. Midseason.

'P.J.M.': −20°F. ARS rating 4/5. 4 feet. Flowers lavender-pink. Early.

'Roseum Elegans': −25°F. ARS rating 2/4. 6 feet. Flowers rose-lilac. Mid- to late season.

'Scintillation': −10°F. ARS rating 4/5. 5 feet. Flowers pastel-pink. Midseason.

'Unique': 0°F. ARS rating 3/5. 4 feet. Flowers light cream-yellow. Early to midseason.

'Windbeam': −25°F. ARS rating 4/3. 4 feet. Flowers white to light pink. Early to midseason.

How to grow: Rhododendrons and azaleas require a fertile acid soil that drains rapidly. Waterlogging for only a few hours may be fatal. If drainage is questionable, plant in either raised beds or mounds. Add organic matter such as peat moss, ground bark, or compost to heavy soils to improve drainage. A soil mix of 50 percent peat moss or ground bark, or 50 percent sand and 50 percent garden loam is ideal.

These shrubs are surface-rooted and therefore enjoy a mulch of organic matter such as fir bark or wood chips. Do not hoe the soil around azaleas or rhododendrons.

Water rhododendrons and azaleas regularly. Any dry period will affect blossoming. Fertilize with acid fertilizer according to the package directions, generally immediately after bloom and every month during the growing season.

Rhododendrons and azaleas do not like wind, and should be planted in sheltered areas or be protected from prevailing winds by other plants. Light shade or half a day of sun is best; some varieties tolerate full sun.

Many varieties of rhododendrons and azaleas may be grown with great success in containers, in which soil is easily modified. Container-growing allows these acid-loving plants to be grown in areas with alkaline soil.

The most troublesome rhododendron pest is root weevil. The larvae feed on roots, the adults on the leaves. Common azalea pests include lacebug and scale.

The landscape uses for rhododendrons and azaleas *(Rhododendron sp.)* are unlimited in regions where their growth needs can be met.

'Scintillation' *(Rhododendron sp.)*

Floribunda rose 'Bahia' (*Rosa* hybrid)

Rosemary (*Rosmarinus officinalis*) is a dense shrub with many growth habits. Blue flowers are borne in winter or spring.

Rosa

Rose

Zones: 5-10.
Deciduous or semievergreen.

Roses inspire the devotion of gardeners worldwide because their flowers are unmatched in color, fragrance, and form. For ease of identification, roses are placed in classes by similarity in flowering and shrub size. Most roses are grown as flower-bed plants for their magnificient blossoms that make excellent cut flowers. Two classes also make top-rated landscape shrubs.

Floribunda roses usually grow 2 to 4 feet tall but may reach 6 feet. They are hardy and disease-resistant. Flowers are profuse, borne in heads or clustered groups all summer. Low and bushy shrubs, floribundas make excellent colorful barrier hedges or accent plants in a border planting. Many top-rated varieties in a range of flower colors are available.

Polyantha roses are low shrubby plants that bear masses of 2-inch-wide flowers almost continuously. Flower colors include shades of pink and orange. Use as low hedges or to line walks and driveways.

These roses are hardy, tough plants that will flower and grow if their basic needs are met. Provide a sunny location, regular deep watering, and regular fertilizing. A neutral soil pH is ideal. Roses are hardy to about 18°F. Below that they need a protective layer of insulation in winter. Prune each spring to remove old and weak canes and create an open center. Reduce all branches to one-half their length. Remove faded blossoms.

Roses are susceptible to aphids, scale, spider mites, and mildew.

Rosmarinus officinalis

Rosemary

Zones: 7-10. To 2-6 feet.
Evergreen.

Rosemary is a fragrant-leaved herb that is native to the Mediterranean region. It was grown in Medieval medicinal gardens and is still a favorite herb garden plant today. It is also used for hedges, especially in Southern California's inland or coastal regions. Low-growing and prostrate forms are used as ground covers on dry rocky sites. This dense-branching shrub has narrow, glossy, dark green leaves, with grayish-white undersides. Small, light blue flowers appear in winter and spring.

In cold climates, grow rosemary as an annual, or plant in containers and move indoors during freezing weather. Does well in poor, dry soil in full sun. Tolerates partial shade. Prune to encourage full shape.

'Lockwood de Forest' is a creeping form 2 feet high. Foliage is lighter and brighter than the species; flowers are bluer. Use as a ground cover, in rock and herb gardens, or in planters. 'Fastigiatus' and 'Pyramidalis' are upright forms useful in hedges.

Sarcococca hookerana humilis

Sweet Box

Zones: 7-10. To 15-24 inches.
Evergreen.

Sweet box is a slow-growing, handsomely formed low plant that spreads as far as 8 feet by underground runners. Glossy green, lance-shaped leaves hide the tiny, fragrant white flowers that bloom in early spring. Small, shiny black berries follow in summer. This plant tolerates deep shade and is a valuable shrub for north-facing exposures and entryways, and for greenery under tall shrubs.

Sweet box is an easy-to-grow shrub demanding little attention. Plant in a rich, well-drained soil with plenty of organic matter added. Water regularly. Watch for signs of scale. Spreading growth can be contained by cutting back underground runners. For an unrestrained, lush ground cover, do not prune.

Skimmia

Skimmia japonica

Zones: 6-8. To 4-5 feet.
Evergreen.

This species is a dense shrub with large, glossy evergreen leaves. In spring the plants have a showy bloom of fragrant white-to-cream flowers. Shrubs are either male or female. Females bear a heavy crop of red berries if pollinated by a male. Requires a moist soil high in organic matter. Light to full shade; the farther south, the more shade is required. Adapts to the rigors of urban environments. A top-rated plant for entryways or container growing. Watch for thrips and spider mites.

Spanish Broom

Spartium junceum

Zones: 7-10. To 6-10 feet.
Evergreen.

One of the most drought-hardy and rugged flowering shrubs for warm climates, Spanish broom has sparse, bluish-green leaves and tough branches. It is nearly leafless but has slender, rushlike stems that remain a deep green throughout the year. Spanish broom is most noteworthy from midspring to August when golden-yellow, fragrant, pealike flowers brighten the landscape. In mass plantings, their fragrance permeates the air. Grows upright to 6 to 10 feet, spreading 6 to 8 feet wide.

Although easily controlled in the garden, this plant has naturalized itself to become a weed on open slopes in the western United States. It thrives where soils are poor and well-drained, even on hot, rocky slopes. Spanish broom is an ideal plant for low-maintenance gardens with little summer irrigation. Use as a bright accent with other hardy, flowering shrubs. Pruning back the stems will keep the plant looking neat and encourage compact growth. Remove old branches to the ground. Caterpillars and aphids may pose problems, but the shrub recovers with no permanent damage.

Skimmia *(Skimmia japonica)* bears showy, fragrant, white blooms in spring, followed by bright red berries.

Spanish broom *(Spartium junceum)* is tough and drought-hardy. From midspring to midsummer the nearly leafless evergreen stems are covered by yellow flowers.

47

Spiraeas (*Spiraea sp.*) make striking accent plants. Clouds of tiny flowers appear in spring or summer.

The sweet perfume of lilac blossoms (*Syringa sp.*) in spring is an American garden tradition.

Spiraea
Spiraea

Almost 100 species of deciduous shrubs native in the Northern Hemisphere are included in this genus. Planted as ornamentals for their masses of tiny flowers in late spring or early summer, spiraeas offer a white, pink, or red floral display. Most shrubs, if allowed to grow in their natural form, will soon make an attractive bush with side branches arching and drooping to the ground. Spiraeas thrive in many exposures and on a variety of soils but require plenty of moisture and full sunshine for best bloom.

Spiraea x bumalda
Bumalda Spiraea
Zones: 3-9. To 2-3 feet.
Deciduous.

A dense, twiggy shrub with upright branches. Flowers are white to deep pink. Used in mass and bank plantings, in borders, and low hedges. The cultivar 'Anthony Waterer' is a compact shrub with white to deep pink flowers in midsummer. 'Gold Flame' may grow to 4 feet; new leaves are mottled bronze and orange, turning yellow in summer; flowers, borne in summer, are pink to rosy-red.

Spiraea japonica
Japanese Spiraea
Zones: 6-9. To 6 feet.
Deciduous.

This shrub has stiff upright branches covered with flat clusters of white, pale pink, or deep pink blossoms in June. 'Atrosanguinea' has the deepest red flowers of all spiraeas. 'Alpina' is a dwarf able to grow in Zone 5; it develops into a mound 1 foot high, and bears pink flowers spring to fall. 'Coccinea' is a low plant to 3 feet, bearing crimson flowers that retain their color throughout the heat of summer.

Spiraea prunifolia
Bridal-Wreath
Zones: 5-9. To 9 feet.
Deciduous.

An old-time favorite, this open-growing shrub spreads to 6 to 8 feet. The many-petaled flowers are bright white, opening in mid-spring. 'Plena' is an improved cultivar with a profusion of white, double, buttonlike flowers. Can be kept lower by pruning.

Spiraea x vanhouttei
Vanhoutte Spiraea
Zones: 5-9. To 6 feet.
Deciduous.

This popular and widely planted spiraea produces masses of white flowers covering arching branches in late spring. Use untrimmed as an informal hedge or specimen plant. Resembles a white fountain when in full bloom.

Syringa
Lilac

This genus contains about 30 species of deciduous shrubs or small trees, originally from East Asia, the Himalayas, and southeastern Europe, that are grown as ornamentals for their usually fragrant flowers. Most old-fashioned gardens in the Northeast had at least one lilac bush, and spring would not have seemed like spring without the fragrance of lilac in the garden. Long-lived, a lilac bush is often the only remaining sign of where a farmhouse once stood.

Although they grow in most soils, lilacs do best in a neutral to alkaline soil that is fertile and moist. If a site tends to be acid, limestone should be added. Over-fertilization should be avoided because rank growth can result. Plants growing in full sunlight produce the largest flowers in greatest quantities, but the farther south lilacs are planted, the more they adapt to light shade.

A dozen species and over 500 horticultural selections have been grown in the United States. Many of the various cultivars are difficult to distinguish from one another.

Scale, lilac borer, and mildew can be problems. Control measures for these pests should be initiated as soon as they first show up.

Syringa x chinensis
Chinese Lilac
Zones: 4-7. To 15 feet.
Deciduous.

The first hybrid lilac; recorded about 1777. Fragrant flowers are violet. Densely branched, spreading to 8 feet, Chinese lilac makes an excellent screen.

Syringa vulgaris
Common Lilac
Zones: 3-8. To 20 feet.
Deciduous.

The most widely grown lilac, with a spread to 15 feet. Hundreds of cultivars with fragrant purple, lavender, blue, white, pink, and red flowers have been selected.

Trachelospermum
Star Jasmine
This genus contains 2 species of vining plants that are often used as spreading flowering shrubs.

Trachelospermum asiaticum
Yellow Star Jasmine
Zones: 7-10. To 18-24 inches.
Evergreen.

Yellow star jasmine is less common than the white-flowered star jasmine, *T. jasminoides*. Its fragrant yellowish-white flowers bloom in late spring and early summer. This is the hardiest star jasmine. It has bronzy new growth. Mature leaves are dull deep green. Otherwise, culture and habit are the same as for white-flowered star jasmine.

Trachelospermum jasminoides
Star Jasmine,
Confederate Jasmine
Zones: 8-10. To 18-24 inches.
Evergreen.

Star jasmine is a sprawling shrub for warm climate zones. It becomes a thick carpet on banks, near walkways, or under tall shrubs. Use it as a low mound in raised planters where cascading branches will hang gracefully. The twisted flower petals of the star-shaped flowers form a lacy cover when the

Lilac *(Syringa sp.)* is widely grown and long-lived. Makes an excellent informal hedge for a property border.

Star jasmine *(Trachelospermum jasminoides)* is a sprawling shrub that forms a luxuriant ground cover. Snowy, fragrant flowers cover the plant when in full bloom.

49

Cranberry bush *(Viburnum opulus 'Xanthocarpum')*

David viburnum *(Viburnum davidii)* has dense evergreen foliage and makes a good foundation plant. If pollinated, flowers produce striking blue berries.

plant is in full bloom and their enchanting scent fills the air from spring to summer.

Star jasmine grows to a height of 1-1/2 to 2 feet with a 5-foot spread. Supported as an upright plant it grows as a twining vine that can reach 20 feet. Prune annually in early spring or late fall to encourage new branches and reduce older woody growth.

The shrub is not particular about soil type or windy conditions but needs a moist, well-drained site. Plant in full sun in cool climates and in part shade in areas with hot summer sun.

The form 'Variegatum' has white and green leaves often tinged red. It is somewhat hardier that its parent.

Viburnum

Viburnum

Viburnums are appreciated for their late spring flowers, their brightly colored fall fruit and their handsome foliage. They are durable shrubs grown both in cold and mild climates. Many species and varieties are available.

With few exceptions viburnums tolerate both alkaline and acid soils. They grow well in wet, heavy, fertile soils and some species also tolerate drought. They grow in sun or shade, although evergreen species look better with some shade in hot, dry climates. May be subject to aphid damage.

Burkwood Viburnum
Viburnum x burkwoodii

Zones: 5-10. To 6-12 feet.
Deciduous or evergreen.

An upright spreading shrub, burkwood viburnum tends to be open-growing as a young plant but gradually becomes more dense. Leaves are dark green above with white hairs below and are up to 3-1/2 inches long. Very fragrant flowers in clusters up to 4 inches across open in early spring. Use as a specimen or background plant.

Depending upon the climate, the shrub may be deciduous, or partially to totally evergreen.

David Viburnum
Viburnum davidii

Zones: 7-10. To 1-3 feet.
Evergreen.

This low, spreading shrub from western China is grown for its interesting foliage and metallic turquoise-colored fruit. Deep veins run the length of the thick, leathery, dark green leaves, which are up to 6 inches long and 3 inches wide. Dull white flowers in clusters up to 3 inches wide open from pinkish-red buds. Cross-pollination must take place before the striking berries develop. Another David viburnum can provide the pollen.

Use in foundation plantings and in front of taller shrubs. Combines well with azaleas and ferns in shady, acid soil areas.

Cranberry Bush
Viburnum opulus

Zones: 3-10. To 10-20 feet.
Deciduous.

This shrub has attractive maplelike leaves that turn a beautiful red in autumn. Flat flower clusters are 2 to 5 inches in diameter and are followed by large, glossy red berries. Foliage turns red in fall. 'Compactum' is a low form. 'Xanthocarpum' has creamy-yellow berries. 'Roseum' has snowball-shaped flower clusters but no berries.

Japanese Snowball
Viburnum plicatum

Zones: 4-9. To 12-15 feet.
Deciduous.

A neat, horizontally branching shrub with 2- to 3-inch flower clusters borne in rows along the branches. Leaves turn purplish red before dropping in fall. *Tomentosum* is a similar plant that bears bright red fruit that changes to black. 'Mariesii' has lacy flat flower clusters on horizontal branches.

Laurustinus
Viburnum tinus

Zones: 7-10. To 4-10 feet.
Evergreen.

This native of the Mediterranean region is one of the rare winter-blooming shrubs. Tight, flat clusters of pink buds open to slightly fragrant white flowers as early as November and last into spring. Bright, metallic-blue fruits last through summer. Glossy green, oval leaves are 2 to 3 inches long and cloak the shrub from top to bottom.

May develop mildew in cool, moist climates. Withhold water and fertilizer in late summer to prevent frost-sensitive vigorous growth.

Several varieties of laurustinus are sold. 'Dwarf' grows only 3 to 5 feet tall and wide. 'Robustum', roundleaf laurustinus, has larger leaves and lighter pink flowers than the species; resistant to mildew, it grows in a wide variety of climates and can be trained as a small narrow tree. 'Spring Bouquet' has slightly smaller and darker green foliage than the species. Its compact, upright growth to 6 feet makes it a good hedge plant. Grows in sun or shade; tolerates seashore conditions but may develop mildew.

Viburnum trilobum
American Cranberry Bush
Zones: 2-9. To 10-15 feet.
Deciduous.

This plant is very similar to *V. opulus* and the two are often confused. Fruit makes excellent preserves.

Weigela sp.
Weigela

Zones: 4-9. To 2-7 feet.
Deciduous.

Weigela blooms in late spring and its arching branches are covered with funnel-shaped flowers. They are a favorite of hummingbirds. 'Bristol Ruby' bears ruby-red flowers in spring and again in summer. 'Candida' has pure white flowers. 'Eva Supreme' grows to 4 feet high and has pure red flowers. Plant in full sun in a moist soil.

A rapid grower, weigela is excellent as a hedge, specimen shrub, or in a shrubbery border.

Viburnum *(Viburnum sp.)* are popular shrubs for both cold and mild climates. Variable growth habits make them useful for many landscape purposes.

Weigela *(Weigela sp.)* grows quickly and makes a good hedge, border, or specimen plant. Colorful funnel-shaped flowers borne in spring attract hummingbirds.

Caring for Flowering Shrubs

Flowering shrubs are available from nurseries and garden centers in three forms: bareroot, balled-and-burlapped, and in containers.

Bareroot: These are deciduous shrubs that are dug up while dormant from the field where they were grown and handled with little or no soil around the roots; hence the term "bareroot".

Some plants are available bareroot in fall as soon as leaves drop. Most are available in late winter or early spring as soon as soil is workable and planting can begin. Shrubs ordered from a mail-order nursery are usually bareroot, and are shipped to you at the best spring planting time for your area.

If you cannot plant a bareroot shrub right away, dig a shallow trench or hole in a shaded part of the garden. Lay the roots in the trench and cover them with moist soil. Horticulture jargon for this process is "heeling-in". If weather is cool, bareroot shrubs are safely heeled-in for up to 2 weeks. If the weather is warming and buds begin to swell, you should plant the shrub immediately.

Balled-and-burlapped: Flowering shrubs that do not tolerate bareroot treatment, especially evergreen kinds, are commonly offered balled-and-burlapped. Like bareroot shrubs, these plants are field-grown, but they are dug with the ball of roots and soil intact. The rootball is then wrapped in burlap.

Container-grown: These plants are grown in the metal or plastic container in which you buy them. There are so many advantages to container growing that most of today's flowering shrubs are grown in this manner.

Camellia *(Camellia sp.)*

Mock orange *(Philadelphus sp.)*

One important advantage of container growing is year-round availability. You can plant container-grown flowering shrubs any time the ground is workable, even while in full flower. In fact, it is a good idea to shop for the flowering shrubs you want during their flowering season. Individual plants, even of the same species, vary, and seeing them in bloom assures you of getting the flower shape and color you want.

Your nurseryman will offer to cut the sides of metal containers. This is helpful, but don't accept his offer unless you are sure you can plant the shrub the same day. Rootballs in cut cans dry out quickly, threatening the survival of the shrub. If you do have the sides cut, press the cut sides of the container together and tie them closed with twine to help slow moisture loss.

Lily-of-the-valley shrub *(Pieris japonica)* is a widely adapted plant that blooms in very early spring.

Soil

Soil texture: Texture is determined by the relative quantities of sand, silt, and clay. Soils that are mostly sand have limited water and nutrient reserves but permit generous quantities of air to circulate around roots. Clay soils, in contrast, have plenty of water and nutrient capacity but restrict air. Neither type of soil is necessarily bad but it helps to be aware of their characteristic limitations.

The addition of organic matter—composted bark or sawdust, peat moss, leafmold, and other soil amendments—is the best way to improve either clay or sand soils.

Soil drainage: Drainage should be checked before planting. Fill the planting hole with water, allow it to completely drain, then fill it again and time how long it takes to drain. Water should drain faster than one-quarter inch per hour. If it drains more slowly than that, you have two choices: Plant in raised beds or mounds, or bore through the impervious soil with a post-hole digger until the water drains at an acceptable rate. Then fill the bored hole with soil that has been amended to drain faster.

Soil pH: Chemists measure soil acidity and alkalinity on the pH scale. The scale ranges from 0 to 14, with low numbers indicating acidity and high numbers alkalinity. The midpoint, 7, is neutral.

Most shrubs prefer a slightly acid soil pH, measuring between 6 and 7 on the scale. Some shrubs are referred to as "acid-loving". These include azaleas, rhododendrons, and other plants in their family, the *Ericaceae*. Acid-loving plants must have acid soil or their foliage will become chlorotic (yellow) from lack of iron.

Soil pH may vary slightly from garden to garden but in a given region, the general range is the same. Rainfall and the amount of organic matter in the soil influence the soil's pH. Rain washes natural limestone from soil, increasing its acidity. Thus, areas of high rainfall have the most acid soil, while areas of low rainfall tend to have alkaline soil.

You can determine the pH of your garden soil by using one of the simple test kits available at most garden centers. Or, ask your local county agricultural extension office about university or private laboratory soil tests.

To raise the pH of acid soil from 5.5 to the more desirable 6.5, add ground dolomite limestone, 4 to 8 pounds per 100 square feet. Use less in sandy soil, more in clay soil. Limestone is slow-acting, so apply it 1 or 2 months before planting if possible.

To lower a high pH, add sulfur, iron sulfate, and organic matter to the soil. Sulfur at 2 pounds per 100 square feet will gradually reduce the pH from 7.5 to 6.5. About 4 pounds of iron sulfate per 100 square feet has an equivalent effect. Organic matter of any kind will gradually add to soil acidity as it decomposes.

Planting

The best time to plant bareroot flowering shrubs is late winter or early spring. In the North this means as soon as the soil can be worked. In the South and West a nursery event known as bareroot season—the time when the bareroot plants arrive at the nurseries—signals the beginning of the best planting time. In areas where soil does not freeze, you can plant bareroot flowering shrubs anytime they are dormant—late fall to late winter.

Balled-and-burlapped and container-grown flowering shrubs are best planted in fall or spring. For fall planting in areas where soil freezes, plant early to allow as much time as possible before severe winter weather arrives. Before soil freezes, apply a layer of organic mulch 2 to 3 inches deep (fir bark or composted sawdust, for example) to prevent repeated freezing and thawing of the soil, known as "heaving", which can damage roots.

In the South, where soil does not freeze, balled-and-burlapped and container-grown flowering shrubs can be planted throughout the winter. If you plant in winter, remember that new plants need regular watering even though temperatures are low and that young plants in exposed, windy locations need protection from strong, drying winds. In fact, anytime you plant in winter or summer be prepared to give plants extra care.

SPACING SHRUBS

The most common error in planting shrubs is spacing them too close to each other. In several years they will have grown into each other and will be crowded looking. Shrubs are best spaced according to their mature height and spread. For instance, two shrubs that will each grow 5 feet wide are best planted 5 feet apart. Even though small plants placed 4 to 5 feet apart might look too widely spaced at first, within a few years their branch tips will almost touch. If you want to achieve a quick effect, you might consider closer planting, and plan on removing some of the shrubs when they start to mature and appear crowded.

Shrubs used as privacy hedges should be spaced twice as close as those for borders, because thick crowded growth is your aim. Some open, treelike flowering shrubs are more effective viewed singly as specimen plants rather than as part of a group. Keep these spaced well apart and not in rows or clumps, or use one as a tall accent among low shrubs.

THE PLANTING HOLE

Planting techniques vary depending upon whether you are planting a balled-and-burlapped or a container-grown shrub. But for both types, you should start with a hole that is twice the width of the roots and the same depth.

"Backfill" is gardener's shorthand for the soil that is placed back into the hole after the plant is properly situated. If you are planting a bareroot flowering shrub, backfill with the soil you took out of the planting hole. But if you are planting a container-grown shrub or if the soil you

Soil

Clay soil has smooth texture and retains moisture.

Sandy soil is gritty, loose, and fast-draining.

Loam soil combines the best features of clay and sandy soils.

Planting

1. Mix organic amendment into garden soil to make backfill.

2. Add backfill to planting hole if it is deeper than the rootball.

3. Add water to planting hole to moisten and settle backfill.

4. Loosen roots that the container has forced to coil or circle, and set rootball in planting hole.

5. Add backfill around rootball, firming with your hands as you go.

6. Be sure the original rootball receives ample water the first year after planting.

dug out of the hole is very sandy or heavy clay, amend the soil you dug from the hole. Mix two parts soil with one part organic material such as compost, peat moss, or shredded bark. Use amended soil to refill the hole around the roots. This 2-to-1 mix provides a transition between the usually lightweight container soil mix and heavier garden soil.

PLANTING YOUR FLOWERING SHRUBS

All flowering shrubs should be situated in their planting hole so that the new soil level is the same as the nursery or container soil level. One way to verify original planting depth of a bareroot plant is by looking closely at the bark just above the root system. Usually the proper soil level will be indicated by a change in bark color: it's lighter below ground level and darker above. Once you locate the proper soil level on the trunk, mark it with string or tape so that it is easy to spot as you work. Plant bareroot shrubs by spreading the roots over a low cone of soil in the center of the hole. Try the shrub in various directions until the most attractive side faces the most frequent viewpoint. Fill in the hole.

When planting balled-and-burlapped shrubs, add backfill until the plant rests at the proper level. Fill in and untie the burlap covering after most of the backfill is in place, spreading the burlap over the soil. The burlap will eventually disintegrate, as will wood-fiber containers. Tear away the 1 or 2 inches of container that protrudes above soil level, however.

Pruning after planting: Pruning now is especially important for bareroot and balled-and-burlapped flowering shrubs. These plants have been field dug, losing many roots in the process. Their top growth should be pruned to compensate for lost roots.

Many nurseries cut back bareroot plants when they are sold. If you cannot see that the plant has been cut back, ask the nurseryman; it must be done before spring growth begins.

It is also a good idea to prune container-grown flowering shrubs after planting. It is not unusual for a few roots to be damaged in transplanting. In fact, some gardeners recommend purposefully trimming container plant rootballs in order to stimulate new root growth away from the circular pattern formed by the container.

Watering

After planting, make a low basin with loose soil around the plant to hold water. Make the basin slightly larger than the shrub's original rootball. Water the shrub by filling this basin with water several times a week. It is very important—especially at first—for the rootball to be thoroughly soaked with each watering.

Newly planted flowering shrubs, no matter how drought-tolerant once established, need regular watering their first season. Occasionally a newly planted shrub will die of drought, despite conscientious watering, because the gardener fails to get the rootball adequately soaked. Problems arise when the textures of the rootball and garden soils are different, because the surrounding soil can be adequately watered while the rootball remains dry.

Fertilizing

Most flowering shrubs need very little additional fertilizer. If leaves, especially older leaves, become yellow, it usually indicates the need for additional nitrogen fertilizer. Any good general purpose plant food, such as a 10-10-10 (10% nitrogen, 10% phosphorus, and 10% potassium), will correct the deficiency.

The specific fertilizer product you use will include directions for use, but as a general guide, 4 tablespoons of a 10-10-10 fertilizer for a 4- to 6-foot shrub is plenty.

Fertilizers specifically for "acid-lovers" such as azaleas and rhododendrons are necessary if you live where both soil and water are naturally alkaline.

Mulching

Mulching is one of the best things you can do for your flowering shrubs and your garden in general. A mulch keeps soil cool and encourages delicate feeder roots that cannot tolerate hot soil to explore the more nutritious soil surface. Mulches also help prevent weeds just by covering their seeds. Weeds that do manage to penetrate a mulch layer are easy to pull because the soil around them is loose.

The most common mulches are fir bark, sawdust, pine needles, and compost. Any type of organic material that does not compress and exclude air is a possible mulch. A dense planting of a low-growing ground cover also acts as a mulch.

Apply a mulch right after planting. This will give your planting a finished appearance and help get your flowering shrub off to a good start. Most mulches are best applied about 2 inches deep. You will need seven or eight 2-cubic-foot bags to cover 100 square feet 2 inches deep.

Pruning

Flowering shrubs need pruning to maximize flower display and to rejuvenate growth as well as to control size and shape.

Pruning to renew: Many flowering shrubs are constantly renewing themselves by new branches coming up from below the ground. This is the reason some century-old plants appear to be no older than a fraction of their actual age. One of the most important pruning jobs is to encourage this renewal process by regularly removing the oldest main branches. As you look at a shrub, abelia for instance, you will see many branches coming up from underground. The oldest branches are thicker, harder, and darker colored. Remove a few of these old branches each year to make room for new branches and to stimulate their growth. It is possible to remove all of the old branches at one time, but that is usually not necessary. Remove the old branches by cutting them at

Watering

Drip watering systems are efficient. They apply water directly over roots at a rate soil can absorb.

A basin of firmed soil directs water to roots, however periodic repair is required.

Many types of sprinkler heads are available to use with your garden hose. Easy to move where needed.

Mulching

Bark mulch is available in many sizes. Use uniform-size particles to give plantings a neat appearance.

Rock mulch does not wash away and lasts indefinitely, but does not add humus to soil.

Irregular particles of low-cost shredded bark bind together to form a mulch that will hold well on slopes.

Fertilizing

Spray leaves with foliar fertilizer for fastest results.

Time-release fertilizer pellets provide required nutrients for one to five years, depending on the manufacturer. Read package directions.

Granular fertilizer applied on surface can promote good growth. Do not apply directly over rootball.

ground level. Long-handled lopping shears or a small pruning saw may be necessary.

Pruning for flowers: Study your shrub's flowering habit. Does it bloom in spring, summer, or fall? Do flowers develop from young, fresh growth or growth one or more years old?

If a shrub flowers in spring, prune after flowering. Spring-flowering shrubs, such as lilac, develop flowers on growth that occurred the previous summer. Pruning after flowers fade stimulates rapid regrowth that will bear flowers the next spring. Pruning in late summer or winter will remove next spring's flower buds.

Some flowering shrubs, such as pyracantha, flower in spring on wood two or more years old. These shrubs are usually pruned in late winter before growth begins. Pruning after flowering will not damage the plant, but many berries, which add important color in fall and winter, are lost. Also, pruning in the late dormant season stimulates more growth and, eventually, more flowers.

Shrubs that flower in summer or fall are best pruned in late winter or early spring before growth begins. Summer-flowering crape myrtle is an example. Its flowers develop on new growth that begins in spring. Flower buds mature and open by midsummer. If you prune crape myrtle during the time of growth and before flowers appear, you are pruning potential flowers away.

Pruning for size and shape: The best way to control size is by thinning. Thinning allows room for side branches, which make the plant bushier. Most thinning is best done with hand pruning clippers, either with a scissor or anvil cutting action. Thin by cutting long branches back to larger branches or to the main stem. Make cuts above an outward-facing bud so new growth is directed away from the shrub's interior. Reduce the number of main branches by cutting them back to the ground. Remove all dead or broken branches and reduce the number of twiggy branches crowding the center of the shrub.

Rejuvenation: Drastic pruning may be necessary for neglected and overgrown shrubs. Most flowering shrubs tolerate being cut back to within 6 to 12 inches above the ground. Straggly, unkempt shrubs are frequently given a new lease on life if cut back, especially if soil is fertilized and deeply watered when the shrub is pruned.

PRUNING SPECIAL SHRUBS

Azaleas: Prune azaleas by pinching tips of the new growth, which begins after flowering and continues into early summer. Pinching stimulates more flowers next spring and a denser more compact plant.

When thinning an azalea, you may cut at any desirable point, not just where branches join. Growth buds are present all along azalea branches and new growth will begin just behind a pruning cut.

Camellias: Camellias are often shaped with hedge clippers, but are more attractive and natural in appearance if thinned.

Flowers will be larger and better formed if flower bud clusters are thinned leaving only the large central bud. Use fingers to snap buds off or pierce extra buds with a pin—they'll gradually die and fall off. Remove seed pods that form after flowers fade.

Rejuvenate overgrown camellias by removing old branches along the main stem, leaving a few leafy branches at the top. As soon as vigorous new growth appears along lower stems, cut the top of the shrub to the desired height.

Rhododendrons: You can prune moderately to thin or maintain size any time of year, but just before or during the flowering season is the best time. Unlike azaleas, rhododendron stems do not bear dormant growth buds. Cut where the branch being removed joins a larger branch. Do not leave stubs.

Remove withered flower clusters by pressing your thumb against the base of the faded flower cluster while holding the stem firmly on the opposite side.

Overgrown rhododendrons can be rejuvenated by cutting main stems back to within 12 to 24 inches above the ground. Cut back one or two main branches a year, rather than removing them all at one time.

Problems and Solutions

Some flowering shrubs are prone to attack by insect pests such as aphids, scale, borers, whiteflies, spider mites, mealybugs, thrips and root weevils. Diseases such as fireblight, scab, and mildew can sometimes be troublesome. General information on specific pests and diseases is included in the encyclopedia section where appropriate. You will also find a column in the care charts on pages 60 to 62 that tells you whether or not a flowering shrub is considered pest-resistant. Using this information as a guide when selecting plants can help keep your garden more problem-free.

Insect pests and diseases can be controlled chemically, physically, or biologically. The tendency in recent years has been away from chemical spraying in favor of physical controls—such as hosing pests off—and biological controls—encouraging useful insects such as ladybugs and lacewings to stay in the garden.

It is beyond the scope of this book to recommend a specific treatment program for every potential insect pest or disease. Effective control techniques vary in different growing regions and can depend on other variable factors such as season and type of weather when treatment is administered.

If you spot symptoms of pests or diseases, such as sudden wilting of flowering shoots, darkened or spotted leaves, cottony masses, dead branches, or unusual sloughing of trunk bark, cut off a small portion of the infected plant, and take the cutting to your garden center. Your nurseryman can usually identify the problem and suggest treatment.

Pruning

An overgrown shrub will lose vigor and bloom less if it becomes too dense.

Rejuvenate by cutting out oldest stems at ground level, after blooming in spring.

Remove faded flowers from lilacs to improve vigor and appearance.

Make pruning cuts above an outward-facing bud to direct new growth outward.

Pinching back branch tips encourages branches to form lower down on stems.

Remove spent rhododendron blossoms, being careful of nearby growth buds.

Problems and Solutions

Take advantage of the gardening expertise available at your local garden center.

Aphids are common pests responsible for damaging flowers and young shoots and for the sticky "drip" from some plants.

Before spraying with any insecticide, read the entire product label and follow the manufacturer's directions carefully.

Planting and Care of Flowering Shrubs

This chart presents in quick-reference form basic information about the planting requirements and follow-up care for each of the top-rated flowering shrubs discussed in this book. It is an easy guide to help you determine what conditions and care procedures the flowering shrubs you select for your garden will need to grow successfully. If a shrub has varieties that are pest-resistant, it is listed as a pest-resistant plant.

PLANT NAME	Exposure			Water			Soil					Fertilizer			Pruning			Pest Resistant
	Sun	Partial Shade	Shade	Plenty	Regular	Drought Tolerant	Acid	Alkaline	Well-drained	Fertile	Infertile	Heavy	Regular	Light	Heading	Thinning	Season	
Abelia x grandiflora	■	■			■	■	■	■	■	■			■	■	■[1]	■	after flowering	yes
Azalea (See Rhododendron sp.)																		
Berberis sp.	■	■		■	■	■	■	■	■	■	■		■	■	■[1]	■	winter	yes
Brunfelsia pauciflora 'Floribunda'		■		■				■		■	■	■				■	spring	yes
Callistemon citrinus	■				■	■	■	■	■	■			■	■	■[1]	■	early spring	yes
Calluna vulgaris	■			■	■		■		■		■			■	■		after flowering	yes
Camellia sp.		■			■		■		■	■		■	■			■	after flowering	yes
Caragana arborescens	■	■		■	■	■	■	■	■	■	■			■	■	■	after flowering	yes
Carissa grandiflora	■	■	■	■	■	■	■	■	■	■	■		■	■		■	spring	yes
Chaenomeles sp.	■			■	■	■	■	■	■	■			■	■		■	after flowering	yes
Convolvulus cneorum	■				■				■		■			■	■	■	spring	yes
Cytisus x praecox	■					■	■	■	■		■			■	■		after flowering	yes
Cytisus racemosus	■					■	■	■	■		■			■		■	after flowering	yes
Cytisus scoparius	■					■	■	■	■		■			■		■	after flowering	yes
Daphne odora		■			■		■	■	■	■			■			■	after flowering	yes
Enkianthus campanulatus		■	■	■	■		■		■	■			■			■	after flowering	yes
Erica sp.	■	■		■	■		■	■[2]	■	■	■		■	■	■		after flowering	yes
Escallonia x exoniensis	■	■			■	■	■	■	■	■			■		■[1]		after flowering	yes
Forsythia x intermedia	■				■		■	■	■	■			■		■[1]	■	after flowering	yes

[1] — Takes shearing; [2] — See encyclopedia; [3] — Pinch tips; [4] — Coastal climates only; [5] — Hot, inland areas

PLANT NAME	Exposure			Water			Soil					Fertilizer			Pruning			Pest Resistant
	Sun	Partial Shade	Shade	Plenty	Regular	Drought Tolerant	Acid	Alkaline	Well-drained	Fertile	Infertile	Heavy	Regular	Light	Heading	Thinning	Season	
Fuchsia sp.		■	■	■			■		■	■		■			■³	■	summer	no
Gardenia jasminoides	■⁴	■	■	■	■		■		■	■		■	■			■	after flowering	yes
Hamamelis x intermedia	■	■			■		■	■	■	■			■		■	■	after flowering	yes
Hebe sp.	■	■		■	■		■	■	■	■			■		■	■	after flowering	yes
Hibiscus rosa-sinensis	■	■⁵		■	■		■	■	■	■		■	■			■	early spring	no
Hibiscus syriacus	■	■			■	■	■	■	■	■			■			■	early spring	yes
Hydrangea sp.	■	■		■	■		■	■	■	■		■	■			■	after flowering	yes
Hypericum calycinum	■	■		■	■		■	■	■	■	■		■		■		early spring	yes
Hypericum 'Hidcote'	■	■		■	■		■	■	■	■			■		■¹	■	early spring	yes
Kolkwitzia amabilis	■	■	■		■	■	■	■	■	■	■		■			■	early spring	yes
Lagerstroemia indica	■			■	■	■		■	■	■			■			■	late winter	no
Lantana sp.	■				■	■	■	■	■	■	■		■	■	■	■	spring	no
Leucothoe fontanesiana		■	■	■	■	■	■		■	■			■		■	■	spring	yes
Lonicera tatarica	■	■			■	■	■	■	■	■	■		■	■	■¹	■	spring	yes
Mahonia aquifolium	■	■	■		■	■	■	■	■	■			■	■	■	■	early spring	yes
Mahonia bealei	■⁴	■	■	■	■		■		■	■		■	■			■	early spring	yes
Mahonia lomariifolia		■			■		■	■	■	■			■			■	early spring	yes
Nandina domestica	■	■	■		■	■	■	■	■	■			■	■	■	■	early spring	yes
Nerium oleander	■				■	■	■	■	■	■	■		■	■	■	■	early spring	yes
Philadelphus sp.	■	■			■		■	■	■	■			■		■	■	after flowering	yes
Photinia x fraseri	■	■			■		■	■	■	■			■		■¹	■	after flowering	no
Pieris sp.	■	■		■	■		■		■	■		■	■			■	after flowering	yes
Pittosporum tobira	■	■			■	■	■	■	■	■			■	■	■	■	after flowering	no
Potentilla fruticosa	■				■	■	■	■	■	■	■			■		■	spring	yes

¹ — Takes shearing; ² — See encyclopedia; ³ — Pinch tips; ⁴ — Coastal climates only; ⁵ — Hot, inland areas

PLANT NAME	Exposure			Water			Soil					Fertilizer			Pruning			Pest Resistant
	Sun	Partial Shade	Shade	Plenty	Regular	Drought Tolerant	Acid	Alkaline	Well-drained	Fertile	Infertile	Heavy	Regular	Light	Heading	Thinning	Season	
Prunus caroliniana	■	■			■	■	■	■	■	■			■	■	■[1]	■	spring	yes
Prunus x cistena	■				■	■	■	■	■	■			■	■		■	late winter	yes
Prunus laurocerasus	■	■			■	■	■	■	■	■			■		■	■	early spring	no
Pyracantha sp.	■				■	■	■	■	■	■			■	■		■	early spring	no
Raphiolepis indica	■	■		■	■	■	■	■	■	■	■			■	■[3]	■	after flowering	yes
Rhododendron sp.	■	■	■	■	■		■		■	■		■	■	■	■	■	after flowering	yes
Rosa sp.	■				■	■	■	■	■	■		■	■			■	early spring	no
Rosmarinus officinalis	■	■			■	■	■	■	■	■	■		■	■	■[1]	■	early spring	yes
Sarcococca hookerana humilis		■	■	■	■		■		■	■			■			■	after flowering	no
Skimmia japonica		■	■	■	■		■		■	■			■		■	■	after flowering	no
Spartium junceum	■					■	■	■			■			■		■	after flowering	yes
Spiraea x bumalda	■				■	■	■	■	■	■	■		■		■	■	winter	yes
Spiraea japonica	■				■	■	■	■	■	■	■		■		■	■	winter	yes
Spiraea prunifolia	■				■	■	■	■	■	■	■		■		■	■	after flowering	yes
Spiraea x vanhouttei	■	■			■		■	■	■	■			■	■		■	after flowering	yes
Syringa sp.	■	■			■	■	■	■	■	■			■			■	after flowering	no
Trachelospermum sp.	■	■[5]		■	■		■	■	■	■			■		■	■	early spring	no
Viburnum x burkwoodii	■	■			■		■	■	■	■			■			■	after flowering	yes
Viburnum davidii	■	■			■		■	■	■	■			■		■	■	after flowering	yes
Viburnum opulus	■	■			■		■	■	■	■			■			■	after flowering	no
Viburnum plicatum	■	■			■		■	■	■	■			■			■	after flowering	yes
Viburnum tinus	■	■			■		■	■	■	■			■		■	■	spring	yes
Viburnum trilobum	■	■			■		■	■	■	■			■			■	after flowering	yes
Weigela sp.	■				■		■	■	■	■			■			■	after flowering	yes

[1] — Takes shearing; [2] — See encyclopedia; [3] — Pinch tips; [4] — Coastal climates only; [5] — Hot, inland areas

Name Cross-Reference

A plant can have many common names but has only one proper botanical name. This list matches common names with their proper botanical names. The parts of a botanical name are the *genus, species,* and *cultivar* (or variety). The genus name signifies the general group to which the plant belongs, and together with the species name describes a particular plant. The cultivar is the name in quotes. An "x" indicates the plant is a hybrid.

Common Name	Botanical Name
Aaron's-Beard	*Hypericum calycinum*
Abelia, Glossy	*Abelia x grandiflora*
Althaea, Shrub	*Hibiscus syriacus*
Andromeda	*Pieris sp.*
Andromeda, Mountain	*Pieris floribunda*
Azalea	*Rhododendron* hybrids
Barberry	*Berberis sp.*
Barberry, Japanese	*Berberis thunbergii*
Barberry, Mentor	*Berberis x mentorensis*
Barberry, Wintergreen	*Berberis julianae*
Beautybush	*Kolkwitzia amabilis*
Bottlebrush, Lemon	*Callistemon citrinus*
Bridal-Wreath	*Spiraea prunifolia*
Broom	*Cytisus sp.*
Broom, Scotch	*Cytisus scoparius*
Broom, Spanish	*Spartium junceum*
Broom, Warminster	*Cytisus x praecox*
Camellia, Japanese	*Camellia japonica*
Camellia, Sasanqua	*Camellia sasanqua*
Carolina Cherry Laurel	*Prunus caroliniana*
Cherry, Purple-Leaf Sand	*Prunus x cistena*
Cinquefoil, Shrubby	*Potentilla fruticosa*
Cranberry Bush	*Viburnum opulus*
Cranberry Bush, American	*Viburnum trilobum*
Crape Myrtle	*Lagerstroemia indica*
Creeping St. John's-Wort	*Hypericum calycinum*
Daphne, Winter	*Daphe odora*
Enkianthus	*Enkianthus campanulatus*
Escallonia	*Escallonia x exoniensis*
Fetterbush	*Pieris floribunda*
Firethorn	*Pyracantha sp.*
Firethorn, Formosa	*Pyracantha koidzumii*
Firethorn, Narrowleaf	*Pyracantha angustifolia*
Firethorn, Scarlet	*Pyracantha coccinea*
Firethorn, Tiny Tim	*Pyracantha 'Tiny Tim'*
Flowering Fruit	*Prunus sp.*
Forsythia, Border	*Forsythia x intermedia*
Fuchsia, Common	*Fuchsia x hybrida*
Fuchsia, Hardy	*Fuchsia magellanica*
Gardenia	*Gardenia jasminoides*
Heath, Darley	*Erica x darleyensis*
Heath, Spring	*Erica carnea*
Heather, Scotch	*Calluna vulgaris*
Heavenly Bamboo	*Nandina domestica*
Hebe	*Hebe sp.*
Hibiscus, Chinese	*Hibiscus rosa-sinensis*
Hibiscus, Tropical	*Hibiscus rosa-sinensis*
Hills-of-Snow	*Hydrangea arborescens*
Holly-Grape, Chinese	*Mahonia lomariifolia*
Honeysuckle, Tatarian	*Lonicera tatarica*
Hydrangea, Big-Leaf	*Hydrangea macrophylla*
Hydrangea, Oakleaf	*Hydrangea quercifolia*
Hydrangea, Panicle	*Hydrangea paniculata*
Hydrangea, Peegee	*Hydrangea paniculata*
Hydrangea, Smooth	*Hydrangea arborescens*
Hypericum, Hidcote	*Hypericum 'Hidcote'*
Indian Hawthorn	*Raphiolepis indica*
Jasmine, Confederate	*Trachelospermum jasminoides*
Jasmine, Star	*Trachelospermum jasminoides*
Lantana, Bush	*Lantana camara*
Lantana, Trailing	*Lantana montevidensis*
Laurel, English	*Prunus laurocerasus*
Laurustinus	*Viburnum tinus*
Leucothoe, Drooping	*Leucothoe fontanesiana*
Lilac, Chinese	*Syringa x chinensis*
Lilac, Common	*Syringa vulgaris*
Lily-of-the-Valley Shrub	*Pieris japonica*
Mahonia, Leatherleaf	*Mahonia bealei*
Mock Orange	*Philadelphus sp., Pittosporum tobira*
Mock Orange, Lemoine	*Philadelphus x lemoinei*
Mock Orange, Sweet	*Philadelphus coronarius*
Mock Orange, Virginalis	*Philadelphus x virginalis*
Morning-Glory, Bush	*Convolvulus cneorum*
Natal Plum	*Carissa grandiflora*
Oleander	*Nerium oleander*
Oregon Grape	*Mahonia aquifolium*
Pea Tree	*Caragana arborescens*
Photinia, Red-Tip	*Photinia x fraseri*
Pieris	*Pieris sp.*
Pieris, Japanese	*Pieris japonica*
Plum, Dwarf Red-Leaf	*Prunus x cistena*
Prunus	*Prunus sp.*
Pyracantha	*Pyracantha sp.*
Quince, Flowering	*Chaenomeles sp.*
Rhododendron	*Rhododendron* hybrids
Rose	*Rosa* hybrids
Rosemary	*Rosmarinus officinalis*
Rose-of-Sharon	*Hibiscus syriacus*
Scotch Broom	*Cytisus scoparius*
Siberian Pea Shrub	*Caragana arborescens*
Skimmia	*Skimmia japonica*
Snowball, Japanese	*Viburnum plicatum*
Spiraea	*Spiraea sp.*
Spiraea, Bumalda	*Spiraea x bumalda*
Spiraea, Japanese	*Spiraea japonica*
Spiraea, Vanhoutte	*Spiraea x vanhouttei*
St. John's-Wort	*Hypericum sp.*
Star Jasmine	*Trachelospermum jasminoides*
Star Jasmine, Yellow	*Trachelospermum asiaticum*
Sweet Box	*Sarcococca hookerana humilis*
Tobira	*Pittosporum tobira*
Viburnum, Burkwood	*Viburnum x burkwoodii*
Viburnum, David	*Viburnum davidii*
Weigela	*Weigela sp.*
Witch Hazel	*Hamamelis x intermedia*
Yesterday-Today-and-Tomorrow	*Brunfelsia pauciflora 'Floribunda'*

Index

Main plant listings indicated by bold numbers.